HOW TO
WRITE A
BOOK
PROPOSAL

MICHAEL LARSEN

WRITER'S DIGEST BOOKS
CINCINNATI, OHIO

Dedication

For Elizabeth, who learned the hard way about the perils of accepting a very short proposal with no outline or sample chapter.

How to Write a Book Proposal. Copyright © 1997 by Michael Larsen. Printed and bound in the United States of America. All rights reserved. No part of this book may be reproduced in any form or by any electronic or mechanical means including information storage and retrieval systems without permission in writing from the publisher, except by a reviewer, who may quote brief passages in a review. Published by Writer's Digest Books, an imprint of F&W Publications, Inc., 1507 Dana Avenue, Cincinnati, Ohio 45207. (800) 289-0963. Second edition.

Other fine Writer's Digest Books are available from your local bookstore or direct from the publisher.

Visit our Web site at www.writersdigest.com for information on more resources for writers.

To receive a free weekly E-mail newsletter delivering tips and updates about writing and about Writer's Digest products, send an E-mail with the message "Subscribe Newsletter" to newsletter-request@writersdigest.com or register directly at our Web site at www.writersdigest.com.

04 03 02 01   8 7 6

Library of Congress Cataloging-in-Publication Data

Larsen, Michael.
   How to write a book proposal / by Michael Larsen. — 2nd ed.
     p.   cm.
   Includes bibliographical references (p.) and index.
   ISBN 0-89879-771-3
   1. Book proposals. I. Title.
PN161.L37   1997
808'.02—dc21   97-18103
                                            CIP

Edited by Roseann S. Biederman and Beth Gylys
Production edited by Amanda Magoto

ABOUT THE AUTHOR

Born and educated in New York, Michael Larsen worked in promotion for three major publishers: William Morrow, Bantam and Pyramid (now Jove). He and his wife Elizabeth Pomada moved to San Francisco in 1970.

They started Michael Larsen/Elizabeth Pomada Literary Agents, Northern California's oldest literary agency, in 1972. Since then, the agency has sold books, mostly by new writers, to more than one hundred publishers. Both principals are members of the Association of Authors' Representatives.

The agency represents book-length fiction and nonfiction for adults. Michael handles most of the agency's nonfiction, Elizabeth most of the fiction.

Michael and Elizabeth give talks on writing, agenting and publishing and present workshops based on this book. They also present talks and seminars called "How to Make Yourself Irresistible to Any Agent or Publisher" based on material in Michael's book on agents for universities, writers' groups and writers' conferences.

Michael is the author of *Literary Agents: What They Do, How They Do It, and How to Find and Work with the Right One for You,* a selection of the Writer's Digest and Quality Paperback book clubs; *The Worry Bead Book: The World's Oldest and Simplest Way to Beat Stress; How to Write with a Collaborator* (with Hal Zina Bennett); all with Elizabeth Pomada: *California Publicity Outlets* (now called *Metro California Media); Painted Ladies: San Francisco's Resplendent Victorians; Daughters of Painted Ladies: America's Resplendent Victorians,* which *Publishers Weekly* chose as one of the best books of the year; *The Painted Ladies Guide to Victorian California; How to Create Your Own Painted Lady: A Comprehensive Guide to Beautifying Your Victorian Home; The Painted Ladies Revisited: San Francisco's Resplendent Victorians Inside and Out; America's Painted Ladies: The Ultimate Celebration of Our Victorians.*

For updates on writing proposals, check out our Web site (http://www.Larsen-Pomada.com). For a free brochure, please send a no. 10 stamped, self-addressed envelope to 1029 Jones Street, San Francisco, California 94109.

ACKNOWLEDGMENTS

FIRST EDITION

Although I accept full responsibility for this book's faults, I am grateful to be able to share any praise for its virtues.

This book sprouted out of a book that editor in chief Carol Cartaino asked me to write. Writer's Digest wanted a book that would provide complete and honest answers to writers' endless questions about agents. It was courageous of her to look West instead of East for such a book, and I appreciate the faith that she, Budge Wallis and Mert Ransdell had in me.

For permission to quote from their proposals, I would like to thank the following writers: David Armstrong, Leon Fletcher, Phyllis Sheon Koppelman, Michael Lillyquist, Len Lyons, John Markoff, Chris Morgan, Arthur Naiman, William Paxson, Joanne Wilkens, Lyn Reese, Michelle Saadi, Fred Setterberg, Randy Shilts, Lynda Van Devanter and Jean Wilkinson. Special thanks go to Charles Rubin for allowing me to use his proposal in its entirety.

By providing me with a forum to teach workshops at the Media Alliance, Annette Dornbos and the membership of the Alliance also contributed to the creation of this book. In appreciation of the opportunity the Alliance has given me as well as its efforts to make the media more open and responsible, I am contributing 10 percent of my income from the book to the Alliance.

I am grateful to rights specialist Barbara Zimmerman for checking the section on permissions.

For reading the book in various stages and for their advice and encouragement, I would like to single out the following editors: Michael Korda, Luther Nichols, Doris Ober, James Raimes and John Thornton; these writers: William Paxson and Kary Schulman; and these agents: Marcia Amsterdam, Arthur Orrmont, Charlotte Sheedy and Oscar Collier; and, of course, my agent, Peter Skolnik.

I hope that every writer has the opportunity to work with an editor as conscientious as Beth Franks. I admit I didn't relish making all the changes that she, her colleague Howard Wells, and copyeditor Bill Betts suggested, but must also admit their recommendations improved the book greatly. So on your behalf as well as mine, I'd like to thank them. Thanks also to production editor Joan Bless for marshaling the manuscript into book form.

My lasting gratitude also goes to my family—my brother Ray and his wife, Maryanne, my sister-in-law Carol Larsen, Rita Pomada, Alberta Cooper and Sally Ross—for their valuable, continuing support.

I am lucky to have as my helpmate my partner Elizabeth Pomada, who indeed helped me every step of the way, including reading the manuscript in more incarnations than she deserved to endure. Neither words nor royalties can repay her contribution to my work and my life. A little place in Nice overlooking the Mediterranean might help, so if you hear about one, let me know.

SECOND EDITION

This book will be judged by clients whom I hope to inspire to do their best work, and agents and editors who I hope will recommend it. So revising it was a formidable challenge.

The writers around the country who have told me either at conferences or in letters that they used the book to write successful proposals helped sustain me. Thousands more will stake their careers on the book's ability to help them get published, and I want it to work even better for them.

Every book creates a different challenge because it involves a unique combination of idea, writer, agent and editor. Our clients and the editors that we sell to continue to be our best teachers, and we thank them for it.

Thanks first to my editor at Writer's Digest Roseann Biederman for her gracious patience, Beth Gylys for her sharp eye and editorial rigor and production editor Amanda Magoto for her help in improving the manuscript.

My thanks to the following courageous souls who read the manuscript and whose suggestions improved it greatly: Antonia Anderson, Elise NeeDell Babcock, Hal Zina Bennett, Barry Hampe, Brain Hooper, Adele Horwitz, Robert Masters, Luther Nichols and James Wade; and agents Andree Abecassis, Andrea Brown, AAR and Wendy Keller.

For allowing me to make use of their proposals, many thanks

to Roger and Russell Allred, Lorraine Anderson, Ted Allrich, Linda Ashcroft, Elise NeeDell Babcock, Randall Brink, Krista Cantrell, Steve Capellini, Victoria Collins, Barnaby Conrad, Rick Crandall, Roger Crawford, Francesca De Grandis, Susan and Peter Fenton, Leonard Roy Frank, Barbara Geraghty, Dennis William Hauck, Barry Hampe, Sam Horn, Wayne Lee, Jay Conrad Levinson, Scott Lewis, Rich Melheim, Mark S.A. Smith, Ginita Wall, Frances Weaver, Orvel Ray Wilson and Bill Yenne.

For reviewing portions of the manuscript, my thanks to AAR counsel Ken Norwick. My thanks to ace publicist Rick Frishman of Planned Television Arts for reviewing the chapter on promotion.

For sending their helpful brochure on proposals, I am grateful to AAR colleagues Elizabeth and Edward Knappman. Thanks also to agent Sharon Jarvis for her suggestions. My gratitude also goes to the authors of the other books on writing proposals for what I've learned from them.

As always, for our families—Ray and Maryanne Larsen, Rita Pomada, Carol and Don Kosterka and the rest of the far-flung outposts of support and encouragement that help keep us going—kisses on all your heads.

Last but most, to Elizabeth who sustains me daily as a person, an agent and an author: all my thanks for all my life.

CONTENTS

Markets for your book. Subsidiary rights.
Spin-offs.

PART TWO

Baring the Bones and
Sampling the Steak

view from Madison Avenue. How an agent can help you. Query letters that get results. Entrusting your future to the mails. The ideal review of this book (and yours). The last word.

INTRODUCTION: A LOOK BEFORE YOU LEAP

Book editors and book buyers have an insatiable craving for new writers and new ideas. It is easier than ever to sell a well-conceived, well-written book that people will go into bookstores and buy.

There are also more publishers to approach and more subjects to write about than ever. The size of the publisher you attract for your book will usually depend on the size of the market for your book and your ability to promote it.

The challenge is to get the right proposal to the right editor at the right publisher at the right time. There is no uniform standard for a book proposal. Agents and editors vary in what they want to see. My approach to preparing a proposal has evolved through trial and error since my partner, Elizabeth Pomada, and I started our literary agency in 1972. Since then, we have sold books to more than one hundred publishers.

How to Write a Book Proposal presents not *the* way to write a proposal, but one way—a way that works for our writers and the editors we sell to. This book is not a substitute for trusting your instincts and your common sense.

With two exceptions, one small and one huge, the second edition of the book is basically unchanged. It has new examples, more humor, fresh insights into writing a proposal and a new chapter on selling your proposal.

The small change is the length of the outline. The first edition suggested one page of outline for every chapter, so regardless of whether writers envisioned their chapters being fourteen pages or thirty-four pages, they were submitting a page of outline.

To make the length of the outline relate to the length of the chapter, this edition recommends that writers aim for one *line* of outline for every *page* of manuscript they guesstimate—for example, nineteen lines of outline for a nineteen-page chapter.

The huge change is promotion. The first edition covers it briefly, but an author's promotion plan has become potentially the most important part of most proposals. If selling a book to a large house is the goal, what an author will do to promote the book becomes crucial in determining the editor, publisher and deal for most books.

This book offers you a proven, easy-to-follow method for preparing a proposal that is flexible enough to encompass:

- the wide range of nonfiction subjects
- the diverse approaches to writing about them, such as how-to, humor, reference and illustrated books
- and the options for publishing them with a large or small house in hardcover, trade or mass-market paperback.

It's been said that once your mind has been stretched by a new idea, it can never return to its original size. Writing a proposal gives you the opportunity to increase your knowledge of writing, publishing and your subject. It also enables you to raise your writing ability to a new level. Finishing a proposal is an achievement worth celebrating. By the time your proposal is finished, you will be a better, more professional writer.

If you don't understand something or something else works better for you than what you find here, we'd like to know about it so that we can make the next edition of the book better. Please send us suggestions based on your adventures in Proposal Land.

Please feel free to read the book and write your proposal in any order you wish.

Bon voyage!

HOW TO GET THE MOST OUT OF THIS BOOK

The following suggestions will guarantee your success with *How to Write a Book Proposal*:

- Read it.
- Refer to it as you write your proposal.
- Check the sample proposals and comparable books for help in providing the information your proposal needs.
- Review the book once you've finished writing your proposal to make sure you've included everything about the book and about yourself that publishers need to know.
- Reach out to your professional networks, described in chapter thirteen, for feedback.
- Do a final revision.
- Read the last four chapters of my book on agents for a helpful perspective on writing, agenting and publishing, and your commitment to your career.
- Visit our Web site, http://www.Larsen-Pomada. com, for updates on proposals.

PART ONE

PART ONE

Selling the Sizzle: The Introduction

HOW TO GET PAID TO WRITE YOUR BOOK

If there is a book that you want to read and it hasn't been written yet, then you must write it.
    —Nobel prize-winning author Toni Morrison

Want a million dollars to write a book?
The subject? You can pick one later.
Does this sound like a fantasy? It happened to Bob Woodward, coauthor of *All the President's Men*. The catch is that it happened after his fourth book in a row hit the top of the best-seller list.

Now is an amazing time to be alive and the best time for you to be a writer. You are blessed with more ways to make money from your ideas than ever before. Writing your first book and making it successful can transform your life.

GETTING PAID TO WRITE YOUR BOOK
In *The Insider's Guide to Getting Published*, John Boswell notes that "today fully 90 percent of all nonfiction books sold to trade publishers are acquired on the basis of a proposal alone." If you can prove to a publisher that you can research, organize and write nonfiction, you can get paid to write your book. But it will require a fundamental shift in your thinking from that of a writer with something to say, to that of an author with something to sell.

You have to sell your proposal to an agent or editor by making it irresistible *before* you mail it. The fate of your proposal is sealed with the envelope you mail it in.

An "In the Bleachers" cartoon by Steve Moore shows a jockey sitting at the starting gate saying to himself: "Why am I dressed like this? Who are all these people? What am I doing on a horse? Where *am* I?"

The caption says: "Seconds before the start of the race,

Filipe suffers a mental lapse commonly known among jockeys as 'rider's block.' "

Jockeys may have a problem but writers shouldn't. The world is awash with ideas. The challenge in this bottomless sea of possibilities is for you to raise a sunken treasure—the one idea that, based on

- your ability
- your passion for it
- its promotability
- its commercial potential
- and its potential as a series

is the best idea for you to write about now.

Finding the right focus for your book—neither too broad nor too narrow—is essential.

FOUR STEPS TO TAKE WHEN YOU HAVE AN IDEA
The moment you have the idea for your book, take these four steps immediately:

1. Try the idea out on your writing and "field" networks. Chapter thirteen discusses the value of networks.

2. Check the competition. Appendix one lists six sources for tracking down competitive books.

3. Read all about it. The more you learn, the more you earn. Make yourself an expert on your subject by reading the most important competitive books and going through others to learn what you need to know. One of the many reasons why now is the best time ever to be a writer is that for any kind of book you want to write, models—both bombs and best-sellers—abound.

Also, read books that complement yours. Best-selling books on your subject that won't compete with your book help sell it by proving there's a market for such books. The publishers of these books may buy yours.

4. Write your proposal ASAP. Ideas are in the air, because the raw material for them is in the media. If your book is about a breaking news story or a hot subject that has to come out as soon as possible, you must write your proposal as quickly as you can without sacrificing quality, and sell it before another writer beats you to it or the interest in the subject wanes.

If speed is not crucial, give your idea the benefit of real-world experience by test-marketing it. Chapter twelve describes three ways you can ensure that your proposal will sell by test-marketing your idea.

WHY THIS IS A BREAD-AND-BUTTER BOOK FOR US

This is a bread-and-butter book for Elizabeth and me, and it can be for you, too. Because it's far easier to sell nonfiction than fiction, we make our living by selling mostly nonfiction books, many by first-time authors. Our livelihood depends on the effectiveness of this book. The book describes how our clients help us help them.

Judging from the letters we receive from around the country, the number of copies the book has sold and the agents and editors who recommend it, I believe the book has helped launch the careers of thousands of authors.

If you have a salable idea and can promote your book, this book will help you launch your career. Once you've made the breakthrough into writing books, you can go from book to book and advance to advance as long as you have ideas, and you can write and promote your work.

One of the many reasons why now is the best time to be a writer is there are more options for getting your books published than ever before: large New York houses, regional publishers, small presses and university presses. You can also self-publish your book, an alternative discussed in chapter twelve.

Only the big publishers do a wide enough range of books and pay enough for them for agents to make a living. Books tend to be big or small, best-sellers and everything else, and it's getting harder to sell small books to big publishers.

We represent only books we believe we can sell to major houses. So this book is based on the premise that you want to sell your book for as much money as possible to a New York publisher.

However, if you want to write a book for a small or specialized audience, or you are not yet able to provide the credentials and promotional muscle that big publishers want their authors to have, you have other options. If you will be satisfied with a small or university press, you won't need to be as concerned with your proposal's "ammunition": the promotion plan and an introduction by and quotes from well-known people in the field.

New York publishers want their nonfiction books to have first-year sales of at least fifteen thousand copies. Because of their smaller advances and lower overheads, small presses can publish a book with initial sales of only five thousand copies. So you must set financial as well as literary goals for your books, and write proposals that enable you to reach them.

HOW TO WRITE AN IRRESISTIBLE BOOK PROPOSAL: THE PARTS OF A PROPOSAL

Some writers find it easier to write a book than a proposal. For others, writing the proposal is the most creative part of doing a book. You have the freedom to plan the book in the way that excites you most, without the responsibility for writing it, changing your vision of the book to suit a publisher's needs, and the pressure of a deadline that goes along with a contract.

Although there is no single way to write a proposal, any more than there is to write a book, the following technique has evolved over the last twenty-five years. It is the fastest, easiest way we know to make your proposal rejection-proof and obtain the best editor, publisher and deal for your book. Follow it closely.

Most proposals range from thirty-five to seventy pages. Your proposal will have three parts in a logical sequence. Each part has a goal. You must impress agents and editors enough with each part to convince them to go on to the next.

The following list is an overview of the parts of a proposal:

The introduction

The goals of the introduction are to prove that you have a solid, marketable, practical idea and that you are a pro. The introduction has three parts: overview, resources needed to complete the book and about the author. They give you the opportunity to provide as much ammunition about you and your book as you can muster.

- The overview
    1. The subject hook: the most exciting, compelling thing that you can say that justifies the existence of your book: a quote, event, anecdote, statistic, idea or joke.

The book hook includes 2, 3 and 4:

2. The title: it must tell and sell.
3. The book's selling handle, a sentence that ideally begins "(The title) will be the first book to . . ."
4. The length of the book (and number of illustrations) arrived at by estimating the back matter and outlining the book.
5. The book's other special features: tone, humor, structure, anecdotes, checklists, exercises, sidebars and anything you will do to give the text visual appeal.
6. The name of a well-known authority who will give your book credibility and salability in fifty states who has agreed to write an introduction.
7. What you have done to answer technical or legal questions. If your book covers a specialized subject, name the expert who reviewed it. If your book may present legal problems, name the literary attorney who reviewed it.
8. Back matter: using comparable books as a guide.
9. Markets for the book, starting with largest one.
10. Subsidiary-rights possibilities, starting with the most commercial one.
11. Spin-offs: If your book can be a series or lends itself to sequels, mention the other books.
12. Your promotion plan: In descending order of importance, a list of what you will do to promote your book. For most books aimed at the general public, this list is eight times more important than the contents of the book.
13. A list of books that will compete with and complement yours.

- Resources needed to complete the book
  A list of out-of-pocket expenses totaling $500 or more, such as travel, illustrations, permissions or an introduction, and a round figure for how much they will cost.
- About the author
  Everything you want editors to know about you in descending order of relevance and importance.

The outline

A paragraph to a page of prose outlining every chapter proving that there's a book's worth of material in your idea and you have devised the best structure to organize it. One line of outline for every page of text you guesstimate. For example, nineteen lines of outline for a nineteen-page chapter.

Sample chapters

Sample chapters (one or more, depending on the nature of the book) show an editor how well you can write about the subject. For most books, plan to include the two strongest representative chapters you can send.

MAKING ORDER OUT OF RESEARCH

The following instructions are presented in the order that the editor will read your proposal. You may write your proposal in any order you wish.

Let's go step by step through the process of creating a proposal that will get you the editor, publisher and deal that you want for your book.

SELLING THE SIZZLE: THE INTRODUCTION

Have you ever heard the saying: "To sell the steak, sell the sizzle"? The introduction is the sizzle in your proposal. If the introduction doesn't sell you and your idea, agents and editors won't check the bones—the structure of the book—or sample the steak—a sample of the text.

The first part of your proposal must convince readers that your book will have what it takes to succeed in an increasingly competitive marketplace.

The introduction sets the standard for the tone, style and quality of what follows. It provides thirteen pieces of information which convince an editor you have a salable idea; you can promote it; and, based on your writing and experience, you can write it. Whether you are selling a proposal with a couple of sample chapters, a complete manuscript or a self-published or previously published book, you need an introduction.

So let's start at the beginning of the overview and hook those readers! On to chapter one.

Chapter One

THE SUBJECT HOOK
AND THE BOOK HOOK

Most editors read at only two speeds: slow, when editing a manuscript; and scan, when reading anything else. The editor, therefore, is liable to make a snap judgment on the strength of your first few paragraphs or even your first sentence.

—John Boswell, *The Insider's Guide to Getting Published*

When you go into a bookstore and start reading a book, how many pages do you give it before you decide either to put it back or buy it? Students in our workshops usually agree that the first page is all they need to make a decision. If they like what they read enough to want to turn the page, they buy the book. If not, they keep browsing.

United Press International tells its journalists that if they hook readers with the first six words, they will read the first paragraph. If they read the first paragraph, they will read the first three paragraphs, and if they stay with the story through the first three paragraphs, they'll finish it.

The goal of the first two parts of your overview is to hook your readers to your subject and your book. The book hook and the subject hook do not require subheads.

YOUR SUBJECT HOOK

The last thing we find in making a book is to know what we must put first.

—Blaise Pascal, seventeenth-century French philosopher

Start halfway down page one like a chapter in a book does and type, double-spaced:

Introduction
The Overview

Then in the first paragraph or two of your proposal, hook the editor to your subject with a quote, an event, an idea, a joke, a cartoon or a statistic. Make it the single most exciting thing that you can write about the subject.

A subject hook can also be a compelling anecdote or statistic that grabs the editor's attention, or it can be both—an anecdote that gives rise to the statistic.

For example, if you are writing a how-to book, consider starting with an anecdote about how someone used your technique to solve a problem or improve his or her life. Then provide a statistic, a round but accurate figure, that shows how many more people around the country in that situation need your book.

> ⚡ **HOT TIP** Editors are extremely wary of anything that sounds like exaggeration. If you overstate anything, editors will be suspicious of everything you write.

For a business book, the anecdote might be about how the Wide Open Spaces Company in Wherever, Texas, used your technique and increased its sales by 100 percent in six months. Then you can add how many other companies will benefit from the same approach.

Assuming editors know only as much about the subject as the average reader, you must convince them that the subject warrants a book. Try to make your subject hook grab readers like the lead paragraph in a magazine story.

Here is an excellent example of hooking a reader from Michelle Saadi's proposal for *Claiming Your Share: How to Get Full Payment and Protect Your Rights After an Auto Accident:*

> "After driving for twenty-five years without a single accident, John Smith had his car rear-ended as he stopped for a red light. He suffered neck and back injuries and lost two months of work. Instead of paying Mr. Smith, the other driver's insurance company went to court, convinced the jury Smith had made a panic stop, and won the case. Although he lost $5,000 and was an innocent victim, Smith never recovered a cent from the accident.

According to figures from the National Safety Council and the Insurance Information Institute, John Smith represents the one out of every five drivers who have accidents each year. There are 149 million drivers in this country, and every year they have eighteen million accidents. Although most of these drivers carry insurance, many of the victims in these accidents, like Mr. Smith, recover nothing at all."

⚡ **HOT TIP** Anecdotes humanize a book by presenting a slice of life that readers have experienced or can empathize with. Anecdotes make for more enjoyable, memorable reading than just abstract ideas.

People like to read about other people. That's why anecdotes are an effective way to get your points across. Make them little short stories that pack a wallop by being as humorous, dramatic, inspirational or startling as possible.

For the subject hook, use the anecdote that will have the greatest impact on your readers. An anecdote may take longer than a paragraph to tell. It may require a page or more. The longer your anecdotes are, however, the stronger you have to make them to reward your readers for their time. Be rigorous in using as few words as possible throughout the proposal. Never waste your readers' time.

You may have to finish researching your proposal before you find the nugget of information strong enough to serve as your opening hook. Don't repeat your opening anecdote. Refer to it elsewhere as "the anecdote that begins the proposal."

To sell his self-published humor book, *101 Ways to Get Your Adult Children to Move Out (and Make Them Think it Was Their Idea)*, Rich Melheim just needed the first part of a proposal. To hook the editor to the subject, he used an anecdote that includes one of the 101 ways and at the same time explains the genesis of the book:

"A woman once came to the author for counseling. Her twenty-eight-year-old son and his new bride had just lost their jobs and moved back into her house. She didn't relish the idea of hosting their honeymoon at her dining room table each night when she came home from work. 'It's not working. I love the kids, but I can't have them in my house,' she told the author. 'I'd just like to be able to walk around the place in my underwear again!'

The author told her to start walking around the house in her underwear and they'd be gone.

She did.

They left.

The book was born.

Eleven million 'twenty-somethings' are infesting their parents' homes. Half of America's adult children can be expected to return home at least once. The average stay is six months. Less than a quarter of them pay rent. About half of the 'boomeranged' parents say they enjoy having their little darlings around the house.

The other half, while stumbling over dogs, cats, babies and 'significant others' who don't belong there, find themselves enduring varying degrees of frustration. *101 Ways* is for parents who believe the ends justify the means and are willing to be just bizarre enough to reclaim their homes before their adult children drive them out. The author believes that 'embracing a little insanity is preferable to having it thrust upon you.' "

Statistics alone may suffice if they suggest a large potential market for the book. The numbers in Michelle Saadi's proposal, 149 million drivers and eighteen million accidents, prove that there's a large potential audience for a book on the subject. In Rich Melheim's book, eleven million "twenty-somethings" means there are nearly twice that number of anxious parents.

HOT TIP Avoid the words *I*, *we*, *us* and *our* unless the book is about yourself. Editors are wary of authors who overuse the word *I*; it suggests an ego problem. Also avoid the words *you* and *your* in the introduction and the outline.

The first two parts of the proposal are about the book, not you. You are writing them for the editor, not the book buyer. If you want to address readers directly, as this sentence does, do it in the sample chapters. The most effective way to sell your book is to stick to the subject and the book.

If you are going to write a book about a new method to stop smoking, statistics on how many people smoke and the toll the habit takes in lives, health costs and lost work time will help convince an editor, who is aware of the problem in a general way, that the subject is worth another book.

Using round numbers and naming a reliable source lend credibility to your statement and to you as an authority on the subject. Dates, geography, money, size, the number of people, the growth of a trend—use whatever data will put the subject into context for an editor and prove that there will be wide national interest in the subject when your book comes out.

Wild Child: My Friendship with Jim Morrison is Linda Ashcroft's memoir of her relationship with the rock star, so she wrote her subject hook in the first person. She uses an anecdote that conveys the nature of their relationship and how well she will write about it:

> "On a sunny July day in 1967, Jim Morrison and I sat cross-legged in a Golden Gate Park gully waiting for the wind to raise our Chinese kites.
>
> Jim recalled a story about how when he was four or five, he and his family witnessed an accident in New Mexico in which a Navajo Indian was killed. This first glimpse of death shook Jim, who pleaded with his father to do something. As the family car drove slowly past the accident, Jim felt a blow against his chest. 'I was never the same. I had this other . . . presence in me. My inner music changed. My heartbeat was different. I could *know* things. *Will* things.'
>
> With a single motion, Jim rose to his feet and began a dance drawn from Native American movements, but accompanied himself with a low, bluesy hum straight from the Delta. Only Jim could come so close to falling and right himself so gracefully.
>
> Soon, the wind rose. Jim grinned. At first, I was incredulous, but I was fifteen, and I believed. Jim Morrison could call the wind! After we breathlessly reeled our kites in, Jim leaned down to me and whispered, 'The wind comes up this time every afternoon. Sometimes, the magic is in the timing.' Jim knew the same was true of the rocket he was riding that summer on the flames of 'Light My Fire.'
>
> No one else can write *Wild Child: My Friendship with Jim Morrison*, because I was the teenager for whom Jim wrote, 'Not your mother's or your father's child, but our child.' About the time

of my sixteenth birthday, Jim climbed through my bedroom window in Stockton, California, to give me a white rose, a book of William Carlos Williams's poems and the neatly typed *Wild Child*. Jim was my real father, my big brother and my first boyfriend. I was his child, his friend, his *Natasha*.

As Jim's confidant for four years, I hold the missing pieces to the puzzle that was Jim Morrison. In *Wild Child*, I will reveal his demons and his dreams. Jim was a brilliant, funny, reckless and vulnerable young man who was haunted by a traumatic childhood. In Jim's own words, the book will explain for the first time the truth behind his estrangement from his family, and the meaning behind the imagery of his lyrics and poems."

⚡ HOT TIP A common problem with subject hooks is that they are too long. Writers start discussing the subject and can't stop. Computers make it easy to add copy, but they don't tell us when to stop. One sentence, if it's a compelling statistic, may be all you need.

Say as little as absolutely necessary about the subject. The subject hook has to sell the subject; the rest of the overview sells the book and you. Your outline and writing samples will enable you to tell publishers what you want them to know about the subject.

YOUR TITLE AND SUBTITLE

The right title can go a long way in selling your book. After you hook editors to the subject, hook them with the book hook: a two-sentence paragraph containing three pieces of information.

In the first sentence, give the title and the selling handle for your book. Even though it's on the title page of your proposal, give the full title again here. In the second sentence, indicate the number of pages and illustrations your manuscript will have.

There's a *New Yorker* cartoon that shows a man with his hand extended introducing himself to a woman at a party, and he's saying to her: "Hi. I'm I'm. . . . You'll have to forgive me. I'm terrible with names." Being terrible with names is not an option when it comes to naming your book.

When I worked at Bantam, the editors used to talk about a

> ⚡ **HOT TIP** If the subject of your book lends itself to creating an institutional alliance with a business or nonprofit organization or institution, try to make it happen. Contact likely organizations, starting with the one that will be most valuable for your book, and work your way down the list.
>
> Let's say that you are proposing a book on how to cure headaches. You will have a guaranteed sale if you can obtain permission to call your book *The American Medical Association Guide to Curing Headaches*. The AMA will give the book instant credibility with all of the gatekeepers who come between you and your readers: agents, editors, editorial boards, sales reps, booksellers, librarians, reviewers, buyers of subsidiary rights and book buyers.

Little, Brown novel called *Five Days*. It didn't sell well, so when Bantam published the mass-market edition of the book, they changed the title to *Five Nights*. *Five Days* tells, *Five Nights* sells. This is a timeless example of what a title should be: evocative, intriguing and enticing, appealing as much to the emotions as to the mind. This applies equally to the titles of your chapters.

At one of his writing seminars, veteran journalist Arky Gonzalez described the results of research to determine what article titles on a magazine cover would sell the most copies of the magazine. The two winners: "Proof Found of Personal Immortality" and "Pope's Daughter Found Murdered in Commie Love Nest."

What's in a name? Plenty! A provocative title will help put your book across to agents, editors and book buyers. A symbol or metaphor that captures the essence of the book can crystallize the meaning and structure of the book for you, the editor and the reader.

Roots, the best-seller about Alex Haley's family, is a wonderfully evocative title that also helped Doubleday's art director choose the typeface and color for the jacket.

Bantam's art director came up with such an effective piece of art for the cover of Peter Benchley's best-seller *Jaws* that it was used for the movie.

Another Bantam story: When a writer was stuck for a title, Oscar Dystel, then president of Bantam, asked him, "What's the point of the book in three words, no more, no less?" When the writer replied "quick weight loss," the title for the best-seller, *The Doctor's Quick Weight Loss Diet*, was born.

Passages is another simple, clear idea that was fortunate enough to be enhanced with Milton Glaser's beautiful artwork. Paperback houses usually change cover art because a mass-market book, an impulse item which must grab the attention of browsers, needs harder selling art than a hardcover book. But Glaser's rainbow of ascending steps was so effective that Bantam used it for the paperback edition. Gail Sheehy was able to use the title again for her next best-seller on the subject, *New Passages*.

If it's appropriate for your book, let your imagination run wild and have fun considering all the possibilities. Consider these titles: *How to Pull Strings and Influence Puppets*, *My Indecision is Final* and *Ventriloquism for the Complete Dummy*. AAR member Andrea Brown, who specializes in children's books, finds that the right title is especially important for children's books. Humorous titles like *Cloudy With a Chance of Meatballs* or *The Cat Ate My Swimsuit* sell much better than straightforward titles.

You have to have a creative distance from your book and be a bit of a visionary or have a touch of the poet to come up with a title that excites you. But when you hear it, you'll know immediately. It will be love at first sound!

SEVEN CRITERIA FOR AN EFFECTIVE TITLE

Here are seven questions to ask yourself to see if you have an effective title:

1. Does your title have an impact like the headline of an ad that compels people to read the copy that follows?

2. Does your title sell your solution? Don't sell a problem, sell a solution. Don't sell a question, sell an answer. Make your title positive and empowering. Convince book buyers that you're going to solve their problem.

When one of our writers wanted to write a book called *The Health Food Hustlers*, I suggested that it would be more salable if he called it *The Insider's Guide to Health Foods*, and that title helped sell the proposal.

3. Readers want a how-to book to be a magic pill. They want to follow the directions and enjoy the benefit the title promises. If you're writing a how-to book, is your title the prescription for the cure your book will provide?

4. Does your title work equally well as the title for the presentation you will give to promote the book? The same title for both creates instant synergy. Whether it's to hear you or read your book, you're asking for people's time, which is more valuable than their money. Your title must convince them that it will be time well spent.

5. Does your title use proprietary nomenclature—a way of expressing the idea for your book that makes it yours alone? Jay Conrad Levinson's name has become synonymous with his classic, *Guerrilla Marketing*.

6. Can you use a variation of your title for other books?

7. Does your title broadcast the benefit your book offers so well that it creates an unstoppable urge to buy your book?

Your book may need only a title. One of our books, Karen Lustgarten's *The Complete Guide to Disco Dancing*, didn't need a subtitle to hit the best-seller list. Other books of ours that didn't require subtitles include *Learning to Write Fiction from the Masters*, *The Random House Quotationary* and *The Sierra Club Guide to Safe Drinking Water*. Elizabeth Pomada's

---

HOT TIP When publishing people refer to a title, they only use one or two words, so do as they do: After you give the full title in the book hook, use a shorthand version of it for the rest of your proposal so editors won't have to keep reading it.

Keep your title short and simple, six words or less, and add an explanatory subtitle if you need to. You will also help book buyers who are researching books by subject if the first or second word of your title conveys the subject of the book. Ingram, the nation's largest distributor, gives only the first sixteen letters of a title in their computerized list of books used by booksellers.

book, *Fun Places to Go with Children in Northern California*, has sailed through eight editions.

THE TELL-AND-SELL FACTOR

Your title must bridge the gap between what you're selling and what people are buying. The right title forges a happy marriage between two realities: what your book says and the most compelling way to conceptualize that body of information. Author Susan Sontag has observed that "the role of the writer is to make bouillon cubes out of chicken soup." If your book will be the essence of what you want to say, then the title of it will be the essence of that essence.

Titles for self-help books, books on popular culture—in fact, any book aimed at a mass audience—must have a high "T&S Factor." Together, your title and subtitle must tell and sell: Describe what your book is and motivate book buyers to pick it up off the shelf. Make your title as clear, compact, compelling and commercial as your subject allows.

Note that this approach to titles applies to books intended for a mass audience, not serious reference works, biographies or books proposing a scientific or political theory. The titles of serious books on any subject can tell without trying too hard to sell. People buy them because they want the information. As elsewhere, be guided by comparable books you admire.

The title of this book is a perfect example of an author not taking his own advice. It was my first book, I was too close to the material and it paralyzed my ability to think of a title. If you look in *Books in Print* at all the titles that start with the words "how to," you will be convinced that there should be a law against beginning *any* title with those words! (It's still OK, if not exciting, for subtitles.)

> The golden rule for titles of books and chapters:
> Make your titles tell and sell.

A casual browser will spend only two seconds reading your title. Make your title a big red flag that screams: "Stop and pick me up! You can't live without me! I'm worth twice the price! Take me home now!"

An effective how-to title incorporates the notions of a desirable activity or skill to be learned, a systematic approach to learning it, and if possible, a time within which the reader will acquire the skill. *French Made Simple*, *30 Days to Building a Greater Vocabulary* and *Total Fitness in 30 Minutes a Week* are selling titles. Freelance editor Jim Wade's choice for the greatest title of all time: *How to Win Friends and Influence People*.

What kinds of benefits might the title of a book or chapter convey? Speed, quality, economy or a system consisting of steps readers can take to bring about the change they seek. Using numbers—10 Steps for Curing Health—is a simple way to present a systematic approach and tell readers the structure of your book.

These titles of books we have sold tell and sell. They combine a catchy title and subtitle that convey the benefit the book offers:

> *Catch Your Dog Doing Something Right: How to Train Any Dog in Five Minutes a Day*
>
> *I'm Not as Old as I Used to Be: Reclaiming Your Life in the Second Half*
>
> *How High Can You Bounce? The 9 Keys to Personal Resilience*
>
> *The Royal Treatment: Taking Home the Secrets of the World's Greatest Spas*
>
> *Tongue Fu! How to Deflect, Disarm, and Defuse Any Verbal Conflict.*

WHEN A TITLE BECOMES GENERIC

How important is a title? Critical. Indeed, it is possible to sell a book based on the title all by itself. That's what Cindy and Alan Garner did with their self-published book, Everything Men Know About Women. *Why do I know that the title alone sold the book? Because the book is 120 blank pages. Yet it has already sold well over half a million copies!*

> —John Kremer, *1001 Ways to Market Your Books*

The best thing that can happen to a title is that it becomes generic.

Jay Conrad Levinson self-published a book called *Earning Money Without a Job*. I read a story about him in the business

> ⚡ **HOT TIP** Don't get too far out or poetic with your title. Try it out on your publishing network to see how they respond to it. Don't offer an editor a string of titles to choose from; pick the best one. You can share the others with your editor after your proposal is sold.
>
> Top speaker Joel Weldon advises speakers to appeal to their listeners' needs, values and fears. That's sound advice for writers, too. In your title and every word of your manuscript, align your words with your readers' needs, values and fears. The more you help them, the more they'll help you.

section of the *San Francisco Chronicle*, called him and sold the book for him.

I attended one of Jay's classes during which he handed out a list of ways to make extra money. I brought it home and as I looked it over, I realized it was the outline of a book—*555 Ways to Earn Extra Money* was published the following year.

Then Jay sent me a proposal for a book called *Secrets for Making Big Profits from Your Small Business*, which was based on classes he was teaching for the University of California Berkeley. The proposal included the phrase *guerrilla marketing*. As soon as I saw it, I knew it had to be the title. Jay's title became the subtitle.

Since 1984, Jay's guerrilla tactics—substituting time, energy and imagination for money—have become so much a part of the language that we've seen guerrilla dating, guerrilla decorating and even guerrilla nostalgia!

Guerrilla Marketing led to a newsletter, a syndicated column, a Web site and a CD-ROM. Now there's a growing network of Guerrilla authors presenting seminars around the world and promoting all of the Guerrilla books. They number thirteen at this writing, and there is no end in sight to the series.

This in turn led to Jay becoming a small-business spokesman for Microsoft and writing *Guerrilla Marketing With Technology* one chapter a month for its small-business Web site.

Choose a subject you like to write about and promote, think up a selling title and, like Jay, you will find there are more ways to make money from your ideas than ever before.

Generic Victorians

Shortly after we started our agency, I drove a cab for a while to make up for the royalties we hadn't started earning. Driving a taxi gave me the chance to see parts of the city we hadn't explored. It also enabled me to discover the beautifully painted Victorians that were sprouting up like flowers around the city.

I knew there was a book in them, so I took two sheets of slides and wrote a brief proposal for a book. It took a year and a half to sell. Local publishers said the color photos would make the book too costly to produce. The New York editors said the book was too "regional," the kiss of death for a New York publisher.

Finally, an editor of illustrated books stopped in San Francisco on his way to visit his printer in Japan. After Elizabeth and I drove him around the city to see the houses, he became a believer and risked $6,000 on the first book.

When photographer Morley Baer and I were roaming around San Francisco shooting houses for the book, he suggested that we call it *Painted Ladies*. As soon as he said it, I laughed with delight. It was the perfect title. We knew we needed a subtitle, and *San Francisco's* _____ *Victorians* was the logical choice, but we were stuck for the right adjective. Our editor was right on target with the word *resplendent*.

The first book, published in 1978, started a national trend that led to five more books with more to come. The words *painted ladies* have become generic for multicolored Victorians.

If you can't think of the best title for your book, perhaps your agent or editor will, or you will as you are writing the book. Consider having a contest offering your networks a prize and an acknowledgment if the title they submit is used.

Titles often change in the course of writing and producing a book. If you're lucky, you will settle on the title that you, your editor and the S&M crowd (sales and marketing) agree will create the strongest response on bookstore shelves.

For more tips on titles, try the fifteen rules in *Book Blitz: Getting Your Book in the News* by Barbara Gaughen and Ernest Weckbaugh.

Mystery novelist Raymond Chandler solved the mystery of what makes an effective title when he said "a good title is the title of a successful book." If you come up with a good title for your book, you will be well on your way to selling it. Happy hunting!

YOUR SELLING HANDLE

If you can't describe a book in one or two pithy sentences that would make you or my mother want to read it, then of course you can't sell it.

> —Michael Korda, editor in chief at Simon & Schuster and a best-selling author

No idea is so complex that it can't be explained simply.

> —Albert Einstein

Stan Gould, who was one of the top San Francisco Bay Area sales reps, once remarked in *Publishers Weekly*: "When we make our calls, we have on the average maybe fourteen seconds per book. . . . What we need is an expeditious, concise, sales-oriented handle that says a lot about it in as few words as possible."

You just had a major insight into the future of your book. You spend six months, twelve months, maybe longer writing your book. Months later, a sales rep takes your publisher's catalog into bookstores and spends fourteen *seconds* selling it!

Sales reps need a one-line selling handle to sell your book. Broadway producer David Belasco's warning to playwrights also applies to you: "If you can't write your idea on the back of my calling card, you don't have a clear idea." It's the "high-concept" idea of the one line of copy in *TV Guide* that will convince viewers to watch the show. The selling handle for your book will be a one-line statement of your literary goal for your book.

The handle may be its thematic or stylistic resemblance to an already successful book or author. Such comparisons are often used because they give booksellers an immediate grasp of a book.

If you plan to write a *Midnight in the Garden of Good and Evil* set in Los Angeles, a business version of *Men are from Mars, Women are from Venus*, or a book in the freewheeling style of Tom Wolfe, an agent or editor will understand immediately what you're selling. You and they will have a model on which to pin your literary and commercial hopes.

THE HOLLYWOOD VERSION:
THE ART OF THE QUICK PITCH

The Hollywood version of this is when a screenwriter tries to pitch a movie by combining two previously successful movies:

"It's gonna be colossal! It's *E.T.* meets *Jurassic Park!*"

You can't just think about what you're selling. You must also think about what readers are buying. Figure out what makes your book unique, what sets it off from the competition. Then create a concise, memorable phrase that conveys your book's content and appeal.

You want to establish what in advertising is called your book's "marketing position." Since the best marketing position a product or service can have is to be the first of its kind, write—if it's true—that your book "will be the first book to. . . ." If you can't be the first book to, be "the only book to. . . ."

⚡ **HOT TIP** Unless you have a complete draft of the manuscript or a self-published book, always use the future tense when you refer to your book since it doesn't exist yet.

Your selling handle must broadcast the benefit readers will gain from your book. If you have trouble coming up with a strong title or selling handle, try this: List the book's substance and benefits in the form of phrases. Then see if you can abstract from them one enticing phrase that captures what your book offers.

> For *Where the Chips May Fall: The Peril and Promise of the Semiconductor Revolution*, John Markoff and Lenny Siegel wrote that it "will be the first book which documents the social, economic and ethical consequences of the explosive growth of the 'miracle chip.'" To illustrate again how titles can change, the final title of this book was *The High Cost of High Tech: The Dark Side of the Chip*.
>
> Arthur Naiman wrote that his book *Every Goy's Guide to Common Jewish Expressions* was "the first humorous yet accurate, concise yet comprehensive handy pocket dictionary of the 450 Jewish words that crop up most frequently in books, conversations, comedy routines, movies and jokes."
>
> In their 107-page proposal for *Home Before Morning: The Story of a Nurse in Vietnam*, Lynda Van Devanter and Christopher Morgan wrote that it "will be the first book to tell the story of a

woman Vietnam veteran, the first book to shed light on this blind spot in our nation's vision."

Of his book *The Mayor of Castro Street: The Life and Times of Harvey Milk*, Randy Shilts wrote that it "will chronicle the rise of both Milk and the gay movement he represented."

The handle in a 161-page proposal for an anthology edited by Lyn Reese, Jean Wilkinson and Phyllis Sheen Koppelman called *I'm on My Way Running: Women Speak on Coming of Age* was "a collection of writings in which women from different times and cultures reveal the joys and pains of coming of age."

When he proposed *How to Speak Like a Pro*, Leon Fletcher wrote in his ninety-one-page proposal that it "will present step-by-step, practical, platform-tested techniques and tips on how to plan and present effective speeches."

Selling handles vary in length, but as everywhere else in your proposal, the fewer words the better. Aim for fifteen words or less. Editors resist what sounds self-serving. Let your idea, the facts supporting it and your writing make your case.

Unless you or your experience is part of the book, leave yourself out of it. Editors are wary of authors on ego trips. Write about the book, not about yourself. Your proposal is a business plan, not an opportunity to talk about yourself or about what you think you have in common with the editor. After you write the subject hook, unless you are the subject, write about your book.

However, if your knowledge or experience is the basis for the book, you may be able to use one of the following alternatives to begin your book hook:

"Based on the author's x years of experience as an x,"
"Based on x years of research,"
"Based on an article by the author in x,"
"A sequel to the author's previous book."

If your book will contain a number of firsts that will help sell it, set it apart from the competition and impress editors, make a list of them in a sentence after your selling handle. If you're writing an expose, list the newsworthy revelations that your book will contain.

Rick Crandall does an excellent job of proving the timeliness of his self-published book, *Marketing Your Services: For People Who Hate to Sell*, and the market for it. In addition to making the point that almost 80 percent of the country's workers are in the service sector, he wisely pinpoints a vital source of sales: women.

"In a cover story this spring, *Fortune* magazine made a major change in the way they calculate their Fortune 500 to take into account 'a new economy, one much more driven by services.' Tom Peters notes that 79 percent of people now work in the service sector—and as corporate downsizing and small-business entrepreneurship continue to expand, the service sector will continue to grow.

Owners of service businesses have one major problem—they don't know how to market. The vast majority have no training in marketing, they fear personal rejection and many of them feel that marketing is beneath their dignity. People working at IBM or Xerox may get up to two years of intensive training in marketing. Doctors, lawyers and contractors get none!

Twenty years ago, 'putting out a shingle' was enough to get business. Today, there's intense competition in every area. From professional services like accounting and law, to trades like plumbing and construction, service providers need help.

Marketing Your Services: For People Who Hate to Sell provides three keys:

1. It is the first book to deal directly with service providers' resistance to the idea of selling their services. Its ethical, relationship-oriented approach is comfortable for them.
2. It educates service providers who have had no training in marketing—and this is almost all of them.
3. Its marketing approach is designed for services. It shows them many ways to market that they can't object to, like providing better customer service, giving seminars and writing newsletters. It does not base its marketing advice on how products are sold, which is what most books do, including most of those about services.

The book shows service providers that there is more to marketing than selling, and that they do not need to 'hard sell.' It gives service providers hundreds of examples and tools that they can use immediately in seven areas of marketing.

With its emphasis on relationship marketing rather than aggressive or pushy selling, the book appeals strongly to women. Since women buy 70 percent of books and are starting new businesses faster than men, this will be an advantage."

Using hooks to hold readers

By the time you finish writing your proposal, I hope that you will be, in a purely literary sense, a happy hooker. You will need hooks at the beginning of your query letter and your proposal, and at the beginning and end of your chapters. In fact, your first chapter has to hook readers to your book.

> **HOT TIP** Making a list of more than three consecutive elements will make the information easier to read and remember. A list may be a string of words, phrases or sentences. The space around a list draws the eye. You may use lists in your proposal to present:
>
> - your book's benefits
> - the markets for your book
> - competitive books
> - chapter titles
> - your promotion plan.
>
> Here are five tips for effective lists:
>
> - Introduce a list with at least one line of explanatory copy.
> - Use parallel construction.
> - Make lists consistent in tone, style and length.
> - If your list consists of a word or phrases, don't punctuate after each item. End the last item with a period.
> - Unless you're writing a book of lists, don't let your book read like one by using too many of them.

THE LENGTH OF YOUR BOOK

Author Ambrose Bierce said of a volume he found too long: "The covers of this book are too far apart."

The second sentence of your book hook is a sentence giving

the length of your book: "The finished manuscript will contain x pages, including x pages of back matter," if you will have back matter, and if you plan to include illustrations, "x photographs, x drawings, x maps and x charts."

Editors assume illustrations are in black and white unless you indicate otherwise. Since illustrations will be on separate pages, don't count them as manuscript pages. (You will learn how to arrive at these numbers in Part II on preparing the outline.)

Nonfiction manuscripts generally run between 50 and 100,000 words, two hundred and four hundred typewritten, double-spaced pages. Humor books may be a fraction of that length, and biographies five times as long. Illustrated books usually require less text. Make your manuscript as long as you need to do justice to the subject.

However, the longer the manuscript, the higher the cover price, and prices affect sales. Publishers shy away from projects that will be too expensive to produce, resulting in list prices higher than they feel book buyers will tolerate. Also, the length you and the editor agree on will be in your contract, creating a legal obligation for you to fulfill.

It's been said that no good book is ever too long, and no bad book is ever too short. Lower cover prices and shorter reading times are making editors receptive to good, short books.

Another reason why now is the best time to be a writer is that no matter what you are writing about, there are more models for you to emulate than ever. Let successful books in your field help you decide how long to make your book and whether to have back matter and illustrations.

In addition to being able to communicate a convincing sense of herself as an authority in the field, Krista Cantrell had a clear vision of her book and the need for it. Note how Krista implies the market for the book as she opens the proposal with a statistic that will startle any editor who loves animals:

> "In 1992, 4.6 million dogs—12,600 a day—were brought to humane societies across the country. The major reason cited by their families: 'behavior problems.' These owners could not find a source of information to help them solve their dogs' behavior problems.
>
> Based on the author's twenty years of experience as a cognitive animal behaviorist, dog handler and animal communicator, *Catch*

Your Dog Doing Something Right: How to Train Any Dog in Five Minutes a Day will be the first book to demonstrate that when dogs are asked to think, problems disappear. The manuscript will contain 257 pages, including eleven pages of back matter and 114 photos."

⚡ HOT TIP When estimating the number of pages or, as you will later, the number of months it will take you to finish the manuscript, don't give a range such as 200 to 250 pages or six to nine months. Be specific and definite—even though you're not sure. This adds authority and credibility to your words.

Avoid the words *tentative*, *estimated* or *approximately*. Unless you have a finished manuscript, editors know you are guesstimating about time and length.

Even if you have a complete "draft" of your manuscript, write that it will take six months to complete it. The less time it will take you to finish your manuscript, the less an editor may offer for it.

THE BIRTH OF A BOOK

Finished manuscripts are usually not the length guessed at in a proposal. What is important is that you have a clear vision of your book.

One writer wanted to do a how-to book about writing because he felt it would be a great help to writers. He had a four-page brochure he had been sending out with writing instructions, and with new information he had been gathering, he felt it would add up to fifteen pages of manuscript, enough for a chapter in a book he was writing.

But when he revised the material, he had sixty pages of manuscript. He began working with an editor who sent him editorial suggestions. He made them and then the manuscript was eighty-seven pages.

The editor then sent him nine single-spaced pages of corrections. Unhappy but persistent, he trudged on but then found himself with a 137-page manuscript. And then came the copyediting. What was the final result of what started out to be a chapter in a book? You're holding it in your hands! And the second edition is over one hundred pages longer than the first!

SELECTING A FORMAT FOR YOUR BOOK

If you want your book to be a standard-size hardcover or trade paperback, or mass-market book, you don't have to mention the format. If your book needs to be an unusual size, end the book hook by indicating how you envision it. Mentioning a similar book that is successful will help justify your decision.

For example, if you are planning to use tax forms as illustrations, then an 8½″ × 11″ format might be better. However, unless you think a large or unusual size is imperative, present it in a way that suggests you're flexible enough to change your mind if the publisher thinks another format will be more economical or salable. Large-format books are more expensive to produce and harder for booksellers to stock on standard shelves.

One of the positive trends in the business is that publishers will produce a book in whatever format will sell the most copies and will recycle a title in other formats and other media if they think it will sell.

In proposing their humor book of secrets they collected in their newsletter *The Secrets Exchange*, Peter and Susan Fenton invoke the universality of having secrets and the appeal of learning about the secrets of others.

They made their collection more like a book by dividing the secrets into chapters by subject. A book like this can be as long or short as a publisher wishes. Another temptation for a publisher: The authors asked readers for their secrets, so they can produce more books as long as the interest continues. Here is how they hooked their editor:

> "Americans are keeping millions of secrets. Not all of them are deep and dark, the stuff of a horror novel or a Geraldo show. In *I Forgot to Wear Underwear on a Glass-Bottom Boat*, the focus will be on the lighter, brighter side of secrets: the humorous confessions of ordinary people revealed anonymously.
>
> Instead of secrets that make readers squirm in their seats, the book will contain secrets you can smile at. In fact, this will be the first book to focus exclusively on real confessions in a humorous context.
>
> These are the embarrassing, awkward, highly personal but humorous moments that people experience, but would never dare admit publicly. That's why the secret-tellers have been granted com-

plete anonymity. The book will include 120 pages of secrets like:

- The lawyer who's still trick-or-treatin' at age forty-five. He keeps an up-to-date computer file on the best and worst neighborhoods for candy.
- The gardener who is so sensitive she can hear potatoes scream when they're deep-fried. She prefers to let her plants die a 'natural death' on the vine.
- The young woman whose first orgasm put her in the emergency room.
- The college guy who threw up on a twenty-topping pizza—and none of his fraternity brothers even noticed."

THE IMPORTANCE OF A PAGE COUNT

Don't be concerned about the number of pages in the published book. Your publisher will decide that. Just figure out the number of 250-word, double-spaced pages that you will write—25 lines × 10 words a line. That's the number that you control. If you prefer, use a word count instead.

Providing an editor with specific numbers:

- gives a sense of the book's size
- shows that you've thought the project through and conveys the impression that you know what you're doing
- helps editors write their own proposals to buy books, a lengthy computerized form. This is called a P&L or Profit-and-Loss Statement or a proposal-to-publish form.

If you've done an effective selling job with the subject hook and the book hook, you have hooked the agent or editor to the proposal and bought yourself more time for them to go on to the next part of your proposal. Onward!

Chapter Two

SPECIAL FEATURES, AN ALL-STAR INTRODUCTION, AVOIDING TECHNICAL AND LEGAL PROBLEMS, AND BACK MATTER

Communication and information are entertainment, and if you don't understand that, you're not going to communicate.
—Best-selling *Megatrends* author John Naisbitt

THE BOOK'S OTHER SPECIAL FEATURES

The next part of your overview describes other important features the book will provide and its tone. Will the book be humorous, serious, down-to-earth? Will it contain anecdotes? What kind of personality will it have? What themes will it develop?

If what you will illustrate is not already clear, explain it. Visual appeal is an important element in what you buy. Publishers prefer to avoid an endless chain of paragraphs, blocks of copy that aren't inviting to the eye.

Subheads are one way of breaking up copy, illustrations another. Think about how to enhance your book's visual appeal. Sidebars, exercises, checklists, chapter summaries, copy in the margins, boxed and screened information are features that will add to your book's visual appeal and salability. Visual appeal is important in books intended for a wide audience, not serious books. Use similar books as models.

Quotations can also be used to break up the text and enliven the prose. However, beware of "The Term-Paper Effect": including so many quotes that your book reads like a compilation with annotations instead of an original work.

LAUGHING TO LEARN AND EARN

The more you laugh, the more you learn. The more your readers laugh, the more you earn. Best-selling author Norman Cousins believed that "laughter is inner jogging." I believe laughter is chicken soup for the soul.

Most nonfiction will benefit from the judicious use of humor. Unless you're writing an expose or a serious book in which humor will be out of place, the more depressing a subject is, the more a book will benefit from adding humor.

Don't feel that you have to become the next Dave Barry to have humor in your book. Search for material in:

- quote books
- joke books
- books of anecdotes
- biographies of people in your field
- other books about your subject
- cartoon books, although you'll have to pay for permission to use the drawing instead of just the text
- books on popular culture
- and books by humor writers.

If money is no object, hire a comedy writer to create material for your book. Where there's a wit, there's a way.

If you want to use humor, anecdotes or other special features, include them consistently throughout the book. Decide on the number of jokes or anecdotes you would like in a chapter and how best to integrate them.

Whether you use humor, drama, intellectual stimulation or inspirational writing to move your readers, strive to make your book as enjoyable to read as it is informative.

Wayne Lee was specific about his book because it was self-published. Being as specific as you can about what your book will contain even if your book is not written will help convince an editor that you know what you are doing.

> "Twenty-five years after an enthralled nation watched Neil Armstrong plant the American flag on the moon in July 1969, national interest in space flight remains strong. A recent survey conducted by Rockwell International shows that an overwhelming 88 percent of the American public continues to support funding for the space shuttle program and considers space exploration an important part of America's future.
>
> The immense media coverage the summer of the Apollo

Anniversary, the Shoemaker-Levy Comet collision with Jupiter and continuing shuttle flights further demonstrate the public's interest in space.

To Rise From Earth: An Easy to Understand Guide to Space Flight, written by NASA space flight engineer Wayne Lee, will capture the interest of Americans interested in learning about space exploration. The 324-page book is the first that describes the inner workings of space flight and exploration in plain English.

Readers of *To Rise* will find chapters devoted to the subjects of rockets, orbits, space maneuvers, the race to the moon, the space shuttle, the role of satellites in daily life and interplanetary flight with robotic spacecraft.

The book ends with an exciting chapter that describes the methods NASA will use to send astronauts to Mars early in the 21st century. *To Rise* also offers much more than a presentation of theoretical concepts.

For example, articles about the history of space flight, the Challenger accident, the recent Hubble Space Telescope repair mission and flying missions on a tight budget appear in the book.

The author designed the book with a visually appealing layout and included sixty-five pages of drawings he created using computer-aided design tools. Each illustration is self-contained and tells a comprehensive story of the concept it presents. *To Rise* also contains 147 photographs from NASA operations and space missions. This presentation style of no math and many visuals will appeal to readers of all ages eager to learn with as little effort as possible."

DESCRIBING YOUR BOOK'S STRUCTURE

You may want to give your book a superstructure by dividing it into several parts. Dividing a book into parts will help assure you that the different parts of your book fit together harmoniously. It adds to the impression that you have thought your book through well enough to give it a balanced structure.

You will have two opportunities to present the parts of your book:

1. If it will help readers understand your book better, describe what each part of your book will cover with a separate sentence for each part. Be brief to avoid repeating the outline.
2. For most books, just listing the parts of your book in the

list of chapters at the beginning of your outline will suffice. This is how the authors of the sample proposals at the end of this book showed the structure of their books.

⚡ **HOT TIP** Speed kills. Letting yourself get caught in a speed trap may doom your proposal. Doing your proposal right is far more important than doing it fast. Speed is the enemy of quality. Don't send drafts, and don't send the proposal in pieces. Don't suffer from a common affliction: being more anxious to sell your book than you are to write it.

The fate of most proposals is sealed along with the envelope in which they are submitted. Sending anything less than your best work may increase the time it takes to interest an agent and sell the book. Like book buyers, editors are looking for solutions, not problems. The further your proposal is from being 100 percent—as well-conceived and crafted as you can make it—the less enthusiasm editors will have for it, and the less they will pay for it.

Your agent may be forced to sell the book to a less-than-ideal editor and publisher. You may have to settle for thousands of dollars less in your advance and a smaller sense of commitment from your publisher. And a small initial sale usually lowers the prices paid for subsidiary rights.

Rely on your instincts and reliable readers to know when your proposal is as good as you can make it. Then, and not a moment sooner, it is time to see if you are right.

If the structure of your book isn't apparent from the nature of the project or how you have described it, tell readers in a sentence how it will progress. A biography is usually structured chronologically. A how-to book starts with the simplest elements of a skill and flows logically to the advanced aspects of it.

If you are proposing a picture book, describe your vision of the balance between text and illustrations.

Including a list of your book's benefits after describing its special features can be an effective way of proving why your book is needed. Listing benefits is more helpful with a how-to book than a biography or a picture book.

In their proposal for *Guerrilla Trade Show Selling*, Jay

Conrad Levinson, Mark S.A. Smith and Orvel Ray Wilson provided a list of their book's benefits:

> "*Guerrilla Trade Show Selling* will provide the following benefits:
>
> - Shows readers how to avoid image-damaging, business-killing
>   show behavior. Some companies would be better off if they
>   hadn't participated in a trade show.
> - Gives readers control over their trade show sales results. Little
>   is left to chance. Includes ideas to salvage shows with poor
>   exhibit placement, wrong show selected, exhibit doesn't arrive
>   and seven other problem situations.
> - Enables small companies to compete with larger, well-estab-
>   lished competitors. Large competitors often don't prepare their
>   exhibit sales staff properly. A small, well-trained exhibit staff
>   will beat a large, unprepared staff every time.
> - Maximizes the reader's trade show investment. Readers won't
>   waste their marketing budgets. The investment in this book
>   will be repaid thousands of times over.
> - Saves time, money and energy in creating in-house training
>   programs or researching the scattered information on trade
>   show selling. Eliminates the need to hire sales trainers—per-
>   haps inexperienced at trade show selling—or expensive
>   consultants."

You will see another approach to listing benefits in Leonard
Roy Frank's proposal in the next chapter. Keep in mind the
distinction between features and benefits: Features are what
your book contains; benefits are what your book does for your
readers. Features create benefits.

AN ALL-STAR INTRODUCTION
An expert has been defined as "someone from out of town with
slides." Nonetheless, Joann Davis, Editor in Chief of the Eagle
Brook imprint at William Morrow, once advised us to "go for
the experts!" When you buy a book, you expect the author to
be an authority on the subject, or at least to have professional
experience in the field, and as a writer, to write the book.

As the author of your book, you become an expert. But how
do you acquire authority before you write your first book? Here
are three ways to gain the advantages of being an expert:

1. Establish yourself as an expert by getting a degree, working in the field or giving talks and writing articles about the subject.

2. Collaborate with an expert. Finding an authority on a subject or a professional who wants to write a book can be an easy way to break into publishing. Make sure the person is promotable and that, based on the trial marriage of writing the proposal together, you will enjoy a happy working marriage with him or her. Rosalynn Carter admitted that she and Jimmy came closest to a divorce when they collaborated on a book.

3. Get an introduction from an expert. The least effective but easiest and most common way to gain authority is to obtain a commitment for a preface, foreword or introduction from someone whose name will give your book credibility *and* salability in fifty states two years from now.

Because we knew science fiction star Ray Bradbury from the Santa Barbara Writers Conference, we were able to get him to write a foreword for Stan Augarten's *State of the Art: A Photographic History of the Integrated Circuit.*

Like the rest of Ray's writing, his foreword was poetic, passionate and visionary. At about a dollar a word, it was light years from the penny-a-word stories Ray used to receive from science fiction magazines.

The irony is that Ray is not a great fan of computers. He once signed a guest book at the Los Angeles Public Library following Bill Gates, and after signing his name, he added: "I don't do Windows!"

For a book on child care, who would be the ideal person to write your introduction? Until he died in 1998, Dr. Spock. Selling almost fifty million copies of *Baby and Child Care* will make parents pay attention to any child care book with his name on it. So find the closest thing to a Dr. Spock in your field. (If you're writing a book about *Star Trek*, try the other Spock.)

According to speaker and author Sam Horn, best-selling authors receive between fifty and one hundred requests a week to read manuscripts, giving you another reason to start cultivating relationships with opinion-makers in your field.

The less qualified you are to write your book, the more you need experts to vouch for you. If you want to write a book about health, psychology or another subject that requires an academic imprimatur and you don't have an M.D. or a Ph.D., find someone who does to give your book a professional seal of approval. In this case, the person doesn't have to be well known.

If the expert you find is not well known, give his or her credentials, and indicate how long the introduction will be—five hundred words will do. A person's name can have value either because book buyers know it or because the person is affiliated with a well-known business or institution. The CEO of a Fortune 500 company or a professor at Harvard will give a book instant credibility.

The time to approach opinion-makers for an introduction and quotes is after you've written your proposal and shared it with the readers mentioned in chapter thirteen, but before you share it with agents or editors. Your proposal must prove that endorsing your book will be a win-win situation from which you will both benefit.

Commitments for an introduction and quotes from key opinion-makers in your field will be valuable ammunition. If you don't want to approach writers now, list and if they're not well known, identify the people you plan to contact in descending order of their value in selling your book.

The two reasons to ask someone to do an introduction are equally important. The person's stature in the field should lend authority to you and your book. The person's fame should help convince browsers seeing the name on the jacket to buy the book.

Krista Cantrell had all the authority she needed to write her book on dog training, but she was going to add to the book's salability by contacting other authorities in the field:

> "The author will ask the following authorities to write an introduction or a cover quote:
>
> - Elizabeth Marshall Thomas, author of *The Hidden Lives of Dogs*
> - Stanley Coren, psychologist, dog trainer, author of *The Intelligence of Dogs*
> - Jeffrey Moussaieff Masson, author of *When Elephants Weep*."

The person won't usually write anything until he or she has read the completed manuscript. If the person feels strongly enough about the project or you, he or she may do the project for the publicity and an autographed copy of your book. On the other hand, a well-known authority may ask for and deserve a dollar or more a word. You will pay for the introduction after your editor has read it and you receive the acceptance portion of your advance.

Your editor may think an introduction isn't necessary or may have a better suggestion for a person to write it. Perhaps the editor can obtain an introduction from someone the house already publishes, which might save you money.

USING YOUR HOOKS FOR A QUERY LETTER

If you have ever written a query letter for an article, you already have experience capturing an editor's attention about a subject and your article in a few lines. Give your subject hook and your book hook the impact of the opening of a query letter. In fact, to test the waters before submitting your proposal, add:

- the name of a well-known person who has agreed to write an introduction if you have one
- the strongest parts of your promotion plan
- a paragraph about yourself mentioning that you have an x-page proposal for the book, which can be completed in x months, and voila!—you have a query letter ready to mail.

If you've had an impressive article about the subject published, attach it to the letter. If it won't impress readers because of its length, style or the periodical in which it appeared, just mention that you've written it. This at least shows that you've had something published on the subject. Multiple query letters to agents and editors are OK as long as you mention that it's a multiple query.

In addition to testing the waters, you may save yourself time and postage with a phone call or query letter before you submit your proposal. In responding to a query, an agent or editor might suggest a more salable slant for your book.

AVOIDING TECHNICAL AND LEGAL PROBLEMS

*Litigation—that machine which a man enters as a pig
and leaves as a sausage.*

      —Ambrose Bierce, *The Devil's Dictionary*

This part of the overview is only for writers whose books are on specialized subjects or those that may create litigation. If your book will not present technical or legal challenges, say nothing about it. Skip this part of the overview, and go on to the next.

If evaluating your proposal requires a particular expertise, an editor will have a specialist review it. Unless you have absolute confidence in the material, find your own expert to read it first. If you do, indicate who it is.

Publishers receive threatening complaints that, more often than not, are settled without litigation. Nonetheless, they are wary of books that may provoke a suit that may cost more than $100,000 before going to trial. Even if an author is innocent, the cost can be charged to him or her.

Among the potential sources of lawsuits are:

- libeling someone
- invading people's privacy if, for example, you're a lawyer, therapist or physician writing about your clients
- using copyrighted material without permission, if it is required
- revealing government secrets
- including instructions that harm readers.

There's a Mexican curse that says "may your life be filled with lawyers." If you suspect a possible legal problem because of libel, privacy or copyright infringement, you can avoid becoming a victim of this curse by having a literary attorney check the proposal and its supporting documents so you can assure an editor that the attorney you name has reviewed your proposal.

You can obtain the name of an attorney from national writers' organizations or through the following referral services:

Volunteer Lawyers for the Arts
1 East 53 Street
New York, NY 10022
(212) 319-2787

Lawyers for the Creative Arts (LCA)
213 West Institute Place
Chicago, IL 60610
(312) 944-2787

California Lawyers for the Arts
Fort Mason Center, Building B, Room 300
San Francisco, California 94123
(415) 775-7715 or (415) 775-7200

May the only courtroom drama you experience be between covers.

THE BACK MATTER

If books like yours don't have back matter, write nothing about it, and go on to the next part of the overview.

There's a *New Yorker* cartoon that shows a patient on an operating table with a nurse standing over him saying: "They're going to have to take you back to surgery, professor. Dr. Bickel got confused and removed your glossary instead of your appendix."

The last thing to mention about the contents of your book is what comes last: the back matter. List what you will include in the order it will appear:

- appendix
- notes
- glossary
- bibliography
- index

Estimate the number of double-spaced pages each part of your back matter will run, except for the index, and end with the number of back-matter pages you will have.

Use comparable books as a guide and be specific. Librarians like bibliographies, appendices and indexes because they add to the book's value as a research tool. Publishers like to please librarians because school, college and public libraries are major customers.

Writers can usually list all of their back matter in one sentence. However, if you need to describe your book's appendices, use a separate page at the end of the outline to supplement your mention of them here.

The back of your book can also include your bio, a description of your products or services, a request for feedback from readers and how to reach you, but this information doesn't have to be mentioned.

> **HOT TIP** Avoid footnotes in your proposal. They are distracting and will make your proposal read like a term paper. If your book will have footnotes, make them "blind footnotes" that readers can find at the end of the book. If you use them in the sample chapters, include them at the end of the proposal. Asterisks also interrupt the flow of the text. Avoid them except in the sample material.

Your next challenge is to excite agents and editors because of all the lucky book buyers who are waiting to rush into their nearest bookstore to help you earn a living.

Chapter Three

YOUR BOOK'S MARKETS, SUBSIDIARY RIGHTS AND SPIN-OFFS

The best test of truth is the power of the thought to get itself accepted in the competition of the market.
—Supreme Court Justice Oliver Wendell Holmes, Jr.

MARKETS FOR YOUR BOOK

Ted Allrich described the markets for a book that was finally called *The Online Investor: How to Find the Best Stocks Using Your Computer* like this:

> "*Win Big: Think Small* will give everyone with a personal computer a compelling financial incentive to go online. It can be sold in retail bookstores, computer stores, software stores, mail-order catalogs, individual investor newsletters, book and computer clubs.
>
> Owners of personal computers, estimated at over 100 million worldwide, constitute an educated and prosperous market. They constantly seek to maximize use of their computers, particularly to earn money. They are also likely to have the financial means and intellectual curiosity for investing.
>
> In 1993, experts estimated fifty million personal computers were manufactured and distributed worldwide. They expect an increase of 5 percent to 10 percent in 1994. If this book sells to the buyers of only one-half of one percent of this year's personal computer production, it will sell more than 250,000 copies.
>
> Combine the PC users with 51 million individual investors, 84,000 stockbrokers, 17,500 money managers and my immediate family, and the numbers indicate how huge the potential market for this book is. Even discount brokers like Schwab, Fidelity and Quick and Reilly may purchase it as a premium to attract new accounts."

P.S. Because of the book, Ted now has a site on America Online called "The Online Investor" at keyword search: OI.

After you've described your book, tell the editor who will buy it. A book may have four kinds of market channels or ways for your book to reach readers:

- consumer outlets
- course adoptions
- libraries
- special sales.

The more copies editors think your book will sell through these channels, the more they will pay for it. So starting with the largest group of readers, describe the buyers for your book and where they will find it.

Television, a major source of competition for readers' time, provided strong ammunition for Dennis Hauck's self-published book that Penguin called *Haunted Houses: The National Directory: Ghostly Abodes, Sacred Sites, UFO Landings and Other Supernatural Locations*:

"Surveys show that tens of millions of Americans believe in ESP, reincarnation, encounters with angels and similar ideas once thought to be the sole province of 'New Agers.' One out of every four Americans believes ghosts exist, and over twenty million Americans believe they have actually seen a ghost.

Never before have so many Americans believed in the paranormal. More than half of Americans aged eighteen to thirty-five believe that UFOs are real (which, incidentally, is twice the number who believe social security will be around when they retire).

According to *TV Guide*, 'television's hottest trend is reality-based programming targeting unreality.' Dozens of new series and specials on everything from angels to UFOs have premiered in the last year. 'TV is both a shaper and a reflector,' noted Dr. Will Miller, host of NBC's *The Other Side*, 'but first it reflects. The motivation is to respond to cultural trends.' The phenomenal success of Fox's *The X-Files* and best-sellers like *Embraced by the Light* and *The Celestine Prophecy* are further evidence that the new cultural wave is only just beginning.

But the recent wave of TV shows, movies and books devoted to paranormal phenomena are actually part of a larger trend incorporating alternate realities, a realm media analysts call 'hyper-reality.' The trend reflects a deep-seated dissatisfaction with everyday reality and a longing by the general public to get beyond the mundane world into more meaningful, more spiritual experiences.

The National Directory of Haunted Places is a travel guide to the realm of supernatural experience. It will appeal to general readers, leisure travelers, New Age enthusiasts and serious researchers. Because the book is a national directory with a detailed bibliography, there is strong potential for large sales from the $1.5 billion library market. Public libraries are always looking for quality reference books in this area, especially sourcebooks with regional information.

The book even has a built-in market, since most of the two thousand hotels, inns, campgrounds and other establishments mentioned in the book will want their own copies. Nearly a third of the entries are tourist centers with their own gift shops that will want to stock the book. Since the book will be national in scope, there will be opportunities in every state for free publicity and promotions.

In addition, there are over six hundred organizations throughout the United States devoted to the study of the phenomena described in these pages. There is no single database—paper or electronic— that provides them with the scope and wealth of information offered in this work. Most of these organizations have journals with book review sections and mailing lists. The organizational, individual and library sales of this book will provide a continuing market for updated/revised editions."

Consumer outlets

Trade paperbacks and hardcover books are sold through the nation's almost thirty thousand bookstores, thirteen thousand of which do more than half of their business in books. Mass-market paperbacks are displayed on wire racks in 100,000 outlets such as drugstores, airports and supermarkets, as well as bookstores of all kinds.

In addition to authors who sell their own books, new channels for selling books include television channels such as QVC, warehouse clubs and publishers and bookstores that sell online. Online bookstores are an excellent resource for researching other books and promoting your own. They are siphoning off a growing percentage of sales from bookstores, which now account for less than half of the books sold.

Starting with the largest, list those segments of the American public that will buy your book. You can present your book's readership with criteria such as:

- age
- sex
- income ("Upmarket" or "down-market" in marketing lingo. For example, a cookbook called *The Truffle Sniffer's Cookbook* will be "upmarket;" *473 Ways to Use Spam to Stuff a Turkey* will be "down-market.")
- occupation, including the number of professionals in the field
- interest in hobbies or other leisure activities
- marital status
- location
- education
- religious or other beliefs
- membership in organizations
- interest in a sport, hobby or other activity
- statistics on sales of related books, magazines or merchandise
- the growing awareness of the subject because of television, films, advertising or the news or electronic media
- the number of people who have a problem
- attendance at events.

Use round, up-to-date figures that will verify that there's a large enough regional, national or special-interest audience for your book to warrant publishing it. Include sources to lend authority to your statements.

Your librarian will point you to the best sources for the figures you need, and you may be able to find the numbers you need online. One way to suggest a large number of potential readers when you can't provide numbers is to write that the book will appeal to readers "personally or professionally interested in x."

If your book will have "crossover" potential, if it will sell on more than one shelf in a bookstore by appealing to more than one group of consumers, mention it. On the back of trade paperback covers you will see the shelf or shelves where publishers recommend books be stocked. Here are a few examples:

- *Guerrilla Marketing Online: The Entrepreneur's Guide to Earning Profits on the Internet*—Business/Computers
- *Lost Star: The Search for Amelia Earhart*—Biography/History
- *The Sierra Club Guide to Safe Drinking Water*—Health/Environment

A statistic in your subject hook will give an editor a sense of the market for your book. For instance, in the subject hook quoted earlier for *Claiming Your Share*, Michelle Saadi mentions that there are eighteen million accidents a year. She discussed that number in her section on markets.

Figures lend credibility and authority to your assertions, but you may not need them if the number of groups of potential readers you refer to is large enough or if there are obviously enough book buyers in the groups you mention to assure a market for your book.

This is what William Paxson wrote about markets in his proposal for *Write It Now! A Time-Saving Guide to Writing Better Letters, Memos, Reports and More*:

> "The market for this book consists of anyone who writes as part of the daily routine in business, government and nonprofit organizations, or who is self-employed."

Since editors are bandwagon jumpers, if there's a pattern of growth in the numbers you present, mention it. For instance, if you want to write a book about cellular phones, the statistics on the growing number of consumers who are buying them will supply an editor with a powerful incentive to buy the book.

Numbers may not be necessary if you will be approaching an editor who specializes in a subject such as computer books and is therefore familiar with the markets for books on the subject.

As mentioned earlier, women buy 70 percent of books (including those they buy for their husbands and children), so a book that caters to them has a head start. If it's not clear to you what kinds of consumers buy the type of book you are writing, ask your bookseller, librarian or other members of your professional network.

Wayne Lee test-marketed his self-published book on space, so he was able to draw a well-defined portrait of the markets for his book:

> "To gauge the market potential of *To Rise from Earth*, a test was conducted under the sponsorship of the Texas Space Grant Consortium, a nonprofit institution of thirty-one corporations and universities that promotes space education and research. This test involved printing one thousand copies of the book and offering them for sale to individuals and organizations.
>
> Through word-of-mouth alone, all one thousand copies sold in five months. Customers included many individuals without backgrounds in science, parents looking for gifts for their children, sponsors of summer space-education programs for high school and college students, university and high school classes, and a number of science museum gift shops around the country, including the National Air and Space Museum in Washington, DC. A list of organizations who purchased the book is included with this proposal.
>
> The success of the test indicates that a vast market exists for *To Rise* in addition to bookstores. Schools and students represent one of the most lucrative markets for the book. More than fifty million students are enrolled in high school and college in this country. At some time, almost all of these students take science classes that cover space. Many students turn to libraries for further reference.
>
> The material on how space flight works and the history of space exploration will never become dated. This will help make the book appealing to high school, university and public libraries.
>
> Museum gift shops represent another market for *To Rise*. More than three million tourists pass through the visitors' center gates at the NASA Kennedy Space Center in Florida and the NASA Johnson Space Center in Houston, Texas, each year. NASA statistics show that the average family purchases over twenty dollars in merchandise from these gift shops. Both the Johnson and Kennedy space centers' gift-shop directors have expressed an interest in carrying *To Rise*.
>
> The Association of Science and Technology Centers also reports that more than five million people visit the nation's one hundred major science museums every year, all of which have gift shops.
>
> Summer camps geared toward space and science education will provide yet another source of constant purchases. Already, the book has been successfully used in programs for high school students such

as Lift-Off and Spaceship Earth in Texas and the NASA Space Life Sciences Training Program in Florida. The United States Space Academy, popularly known as 'Space Camp,' is evaluating *To Rise* and has expressed an interest in providing the book to its one thousand students annually. Students who return from these education camps are excited about their experiences and will provide a publicity network for the book."

Then list specialty stores such as gourmet shops, music, sporting goods, hardware or stationery stores that sell similar books. Check with stores to see if they can sell your book. If they can, ask them how many such stores there are in the country or how you can find that number, and how they buy their books. You may not find a large selection of books in specialty stores, but if your book has that potential, passing this information along will impress editors.

Course adoptions

If your book will have adoption potential in schools or other institutions, identify the courses and academic levels for which it will be suitable. Naming professors at schools, well known if possible, who are eager to adopt your book and the courses they will use it for will serve you well.

Leonard Roy Frank linked a concise list of readers for his quotation book to a list of the benefits the book will offer them:

> "*The Quotationary* will serve a broad range of casual and serious readers, especially students, teachers, media people, researchers, bibliophiles, thinkers, activists and professionals whose work involves writing and/or public speaking, as:
>
> 1. a highly readable source for inspirational, provocative, instructive and amusing material
> 2. a reliable, easy-to-use reference work for finding the precise wording, authors and sources of quotations
> 3. a storehouse of choice ideas in cross-referenced categories to stimulate thought and imagination generally and thematically
> 4. a catalyst for personal and social change
> 5. a treasure trove for those who experience the joy of recognition and the joy of discovery while exploring the world of ideas

6. a history of ideas, an overview of culture, an enjoyable and relatively easy way to introduce oneself to the wisdom, knowledge, wit and folly of the ages."

Libraries

School, college, public and corporate libraries are collectively a large potential market for books. If your book will have special appeal to any of these libraries, check with librarians and mention it.

Special sales

Special sales are bulk sales to corporations or institutions which might buy large quantities of your book for internal use, to give away or to sell at a reduced price.

A savings and loan in our neighborhood once gave away a series of Bantam's ethnic cookbooks over a period of time to encourage prospective savers to start accounts. A corporation might buy copies of a book on business writing for its employees.

This kind of sale is more likely with a mass-market book than a more expensive trade paperback, more likely with a paperback than a hardcover and more likely still when a company can see the published book.

Noting what kinds of companies use books and discussing this possibility with friends who know marketing will help you decide if your book can generate special sales. Only a small percentage of books are used this way, so don't spend much time investigating it unless you can deliver a sale yourself. Major publishers have sales departments for pursuing special sales.

For *Making Videos for Money: Planning and Producing Information Videos, Commercials and Infomercials*, Barry Hampe cited the increasing number of videomakers and other markets that added to his credibility as an authority on the subject:

"The primary market for the book will be this new wave of videomakers—both working professionals and newcomers to the field—who need help in achieving their goals. In the years ahead, making information videos, commercials and infomercials will be bread and butter for virtually all videomakers.

This market includes professional production people who face the need to expand their skills into new areas and recognize the need for resource information. The book will enable a professionally trained camera operator to structure a video production. As a scriptwriter and video doctor, the author has saved producers who began shooting information videos with no idea how to go about it.

The market includes writers—both those with some experience as scriptwriters moving into a new area and writers whose experience is all in print—who face the need to write the script for an information video, an infomercial or a television commercial.

It also includes newcomers to the field—earnest amateurs or trained professionals—who want to make video productions and don't know how or have started a production and then realized that they don't know what to do.

An important market for the book will be colleges and libraries. Adoption as a college text will give the book legs. Library sales will help make the book profitable.

Video equipment and supply stores can stock the books for sale to their customers.

The book will also attract readers who have discovered the author's previous two books on writing and producing video."

SUBSIDIARY RIGHTS

Books are the seeds and soil from which all other projects spring.
—Laurence Kirschbaum, president, Warner Books

One of the many reasons why now is the best time ever to be a writer is that there are more ways to make money from your ideas than ever. Among the rights you may benefit from are:

- television and feature film rights
- foreign rights—if you can, list countries that will be particularly interested in your book
- first and second serial rights—excerpting the book in newspapers and magazines before and after publication. If you have media contacts and want to sell first serial rights, mention it in your promotion plan.
- audiocassettes and CDs
- videocassettes
- merchandising rights—items such as coffee mugs or T-shirts

- CD-ROMs
- software.

Your publisher will retain the right to sell your book to book clubs, but mention which clubs will be interested in it. *Literary Market Place*, an industry reference book you'll find in libraries, includes a list of clubs.

If you have an agent or plan to use your proposal to find one, the agent may want to keep as many of these rights for you as possible, but mentioning them will add to the editor's sense of excitement about the project's potential.

Merchandising rights usually come into play with certain kinds of books, such as humor books, with an important graphic element that lends itself to translation into other forms and media. Usually only best-sellers create the recognition needed for merchandising sales. Jim Davis's feline friend Garfield, for instance, found his way onto cups, towels and other products. Agent Andrea Brown has found that merchandising can be especially lucrative for children's books.

One hundred companies made one thousand products to tie in with the film version of Michael Crichton's *Jurassic Park*, and they sold more than one billion dollars' worth of them.

Reading *Publishers Weekly* will help keep you abreast of what kinds of rights are being sold, by whom and for how much. Look for products derived from books, and get into the habit of thinking creatively about how to resell your book in media other than books.

A first-time novelist once came to us with a humorous novel about a dying multimillionairess who lives in a penthouse. To go on living, she hires an Indian guru who, at the moment she dies, is going to transfer her soul into the body of her beautiful young nurse.

However, in the excitement of the moment, the guru slips, and the vessel containing the soul of the multimillionairess falls out of her penthouse into the body of a drunken bum in the alley below.

I immediately envisioned Katharine Hepburn and Lee Marvin as perfect for the movie. However, the first producer to see it, bought it, and turned it into a hilarious movie starring Steve Martin and Lily Tomlin called *All of Me*.

Humorous novels by unknown writers are tough to sell, so we were *never* able to sell the book rights. The only money the author made on the book was on the subsidiary rights.

Because there are many opportunities to profit from your ideas, when you're thinking about what to write, take into consideration a book's potential for subsidiary rights. The sample proposals at the end of the book include discussions of subsidiary rights.

SPIN-OFFS

Editors and agents don't want literary one-night stands. They want to discover writers, not just books. Writers who turn out a book a year, each better and more profitable than the last, are the foundation of a successful agency or publisher.

Always look at your ideas in the largest possible way. If your book has the potential to be a series of books, it will make you and your book more important to a publisher. You may be on your way to a multibook deal, which will increase the house's commitment to you and the project.

If you can develop your book into a series on the same subject or with the same structure, begin this section with the statement: "(Title) will be the first in a series of x books including A, B and C." List the books, starting with the most commercial idea, and indicate how many months it will take you to finish each one.

Books often lend themselves to other books on the same subject or with the same structure. Will your book lend itself to sequels?

If you're writing a book for men, are variations for women, children or young adults possible? Writing for children is an art unto itself, but your agent or publisher may be able to find you a collaborator if you need one.

If it's an introductory book, can you write additional books for intermediate and advanced levels?

If your book is directed to corporate types, would it also be useful to entrepreneurs and nonprofit groups?

If you're planning a book that can be adopted for a college course, can you write other versions that can be used in elementary, high school, graduate school, English-as-a-second language classes or the burgeoning field of continuing education?

Although a series of books is an attractive idea, a publisher may hesitate to commit to more than one book, especially by a writer without a track record, unless it promises to be a surefire success. The publisher may prefer to wait to see a complete manuscript or how the first book fares before committing to the next one.

Nonetheless, if your idea lends itself to being extended or recycled in other books, mention them even if you don't want to write them. They will help prove your book's commercial potential. If your first book is successful enough, you may change your mind and decide to write the spin-off books or find a collaborator.

You will have many opportunities to generate ideas and copy for future books. You can use the last page of the book to ask for readers' reactions or experiences. You can also ask for feedback when you give talks and interviews and when you are promoting the book online. Readers will write you to tell about their responses to your book.

HOT TIP One way to set up a two-book deal is to make the last page of your proposal a one-page, single-spaced proposal for your next book. Start with the title, then include a list of chapter titles with one line about each. At the bottom of the page, give the length of the book and how long it will take you to finish it.

Promotion is usually the most challenging and can be the most exciting part of publishing your book. The fate of your book will probably hinge on the next part of your proposal.

Chapter Four

YOUR PROMOTION PLAN

Less than ten percent of the trade books published make money for their publisher.
    —Bill Gates, *The Road Ahead*

M y book will promote itself." We've heard this many times over the years and always envied the innocence of the writers who said it. Sure it's possible for word of mouth to make your book successful, but unless your expectations for your book are small, you wouldn't want to risk your career on it happening with your book.

As you develop your proposal, establish literary and financial goals for your book:

- What kind of publisher do you want to publish it—a large house, a small press or a university press?
- How big an advance do you want for it?
- How many copies do you want your book to sell?

You may answer these questions any way you wish. The only right answers are the answers that work for you. However, your answers must motivate you to produce your best work, and they affect how you prepare your proposal. Your effort in writing and promoting your book must enable you to achieve your goals.

A PERSPECTIVE ON PROMOTION
This book grew from our experience selling books to the major New York houses. That's how we make our living. So the premise of this book is that you want to sell your book to a big house for as much money as you can get.

If you will be happy being published by a small or university press, your promotion plan will be less important because, with lower overheads, small and university presses don't have to sell as many copies as large houses to make a profit. So your promotion plan will not be as important a factor in selling your book.

Best-selling business author Zig Ziglar once said: "A hypocrite is a person who complains about all the sex and violence on his VCR." The chief complaint authors have against their publishers is the lack of promotion.

When *Chicken Soup for the Soul* was published, author Jack Canfield says he had "too much month at the end of the money." He was in debt. But when books arrived in the stores, he visualized crowds flocking in to buy it. Unfortunately, it was, as he put it, "the calm before the calm." Then Jack and his coauthor Mark Victor Hansen spent 90 percent of their time promoting their book for fourteen months until it hit the best-seller list.

No matter who publishes *your* book, think of it as being self-published. The little that publishers do for most books—send out review copies and perhaps contact national shows hoping for a lucky break—they do before publication. If the book takes off, they will promote it to try to sustain its momentum.

If, as is the case more than 90 percent of the time, it doesn't, they're on to the next list. Two months later and forever after, there's just you and your book. If your book maintains a high enough level of sales, there's also your publisher functioning as a distribution service and keeping your book in stores.

As my brother Ray, who's in the toy business, once said: "Business doesn't go, you have to push it." If you are not driven to succeed, you'll be run over by the competition. However, this puts the steering wheel controlling your book's fate in the hands of the person who cares about it the most: you.

It's been said that judgment is what you get from experience, and good judgment is what you get from bad experience. Books tend to be big or small: best-sellers and the rest of the list. The more publishers pay, the more they push, but even a $100,000 advance is no guarantee a big house will promote a book. New authors usually learn through bitter experience the unhappy truths about writing a small book for a big house.

According to a well-known member of the Association of Authors' Representatives who owns a New York agency: "Publishers pay starvation wages to new, inexperienced publicists." Then they inundate them with too many books to publicize.

A Simon & Schuster editor recalled when he was first hired by the house as a publicist, he was assigned sixty books to publicize. Divide sixty into forty hours a week, and then add the high turnover rate caused in part by such working conditions, and you will begin to understand the pressure publicists endure.

Since too many books are published to receive the attention they deserve, publishers focus their attention on those they believe have the greatest potential to repay their effort.

Large houses want authors who are "ready to pop," who already have a high V.Q. or Visibility Quotient. An editor at Warner once asked about an author we were pitching: "Does she have a profile?" Editors at HarperCollins inquire about an author's "national platform."

They are both asking the same question in different ways, because they are both looking for the same thing: a high Visibility Quotient. How visible an author will remain around the country on a continuing basis is an essential factor in deciding whether to acquire a book and for how much.

John Gray and Deepak Chopra are models for successful authors. They are tireless promoters who crisscross the country seizing every opportunity to promote themselves and their books. Are you ready to raise your V.Q.?

Publishers will have a short- and long-term perspective on promotion. They will be especially concerned about maximizing the opportunity for promoting your book during your book's "launch window," the one-month window of opportunity starting on the publication of your book when, one hopes, books are in stores and reviews are appearing.

Beyond that, they'll want you to continue to promote your books as long as you can walk and talk at the same time. Simon & Schuster senior editor Fred Hills once said: "I want authors whose subjects are their professional lives, who are out there hustling forty weeks a year."

For his book on using a computer to invest, Ted Allrich provided a strong promotion plan. At first, publishers were reluctant to buy the book, so Ted created an institutional affiliation with Prodigy, the online service provider. After they made the following commitment, we quickly received two offers.

"On the basis of the proposal, Prodigy, a joint venture between IBM and Sears, is willing to promote it extensively:

1. Purchase twenty-five hundred per month as a premium to attract new members as long as the promotion is effective. In one year, that will be thirty thousand books.
2. Sponsor a seminar in the fall of 1994 in initially four eastern cities for their current and potential subscribers. The author will be one of three or four featured speakers. If these are successful, the seminars will be national. The book will be available for sale at the seminar or bought by Prodigy as a premium.
3. Promote the book online as part of the investment library. Books will be bought by the provider of the library service. There are two million Prodigy subscribers; if half of 1 percent buy the book, that's ten thousand books.
4. A bulletin board for the author where questions can be answered about investing and subscribers can be referred to the book.
5. Distribution of the book in Sears and IBM outlets and wherever Prodigy software is sold.
6. A cover quote by the head of the investment information services of Prodigy who has said Prodigy is willing to use its services to their fullest extent to make the book successful.

While the author welcomes Prodigy's involvement, and acknowledges the databases used on its service are the most affordable and practical for an individual investor, he is writing an independent, objective book about investing. Other services and research databases will be included.

The author understands the importance of a good publicity and marketing campaign for the success of *Win Big: Think Small*. There will be a coordinated effort between the author and the publisher, carefully planned and enthusiastically pursued. The author makes the following commitments:

1. Because the book will be the marketing tool for the author's firm and will help him establish an audience for his next book, software and a newsletter, he will match the publisher's consumer promotion budget up to $x.
2. The author has hired book publicist Blanche Brann, a former

director of publicity for Holt, as his publicity consultant. Prior to Holt, Brann was with Doubleday. She is currently working with Regis McKenna, the acknowledged public relations genius, on publicity for his latest book. The author and Brann will create a press kit and publicity releases.

The press kit will contain a:

Pitch letter
National and Bay Area press releases
"The story behind the book," a short history of how the author
    came to write the book and his dedication to investing
Photograph of the author
Brochure on the author's firm
Any reviews and articles on the book once received
Questions on investing, computing and the stock market for
    the media to ask the author

Print

Magazines: Business, investing and computer magazine coverage: press kits will be sent to all business and computer publications including *Business Week*, *PC Magazine*, *PC World Magazine*, *Money Magazine*, *Fortune*, *Forbes* and its new specialty publication *ASAP*, dedicated to computer users.

Newspapers and newswires: The thirty-five largest metropolitan area business and computer editors will get publicity packets and a book. That package will go also to the nationally syndicated business and technology columnists and feature writers. All other newspapers with a business or computer editor will receive the packet and a response card for requesting the book.

Special-interest publications: Editors of specialty publications for investors such as the American Association of Independent Investors, advisory newsletters such as *Personal Finance*, *The Prudent Speculator* and computer-user newsletters will receive the publicity packet.

Broadcast

Network: A proposal for network and local news will show how the visual presentation with a laptop computer attached to an LCD projector is visually interesting to their investor, computer and business viewers. Ideal programs are CNBC, *Moneyline* and *Wall Street Week*.

    Radio telephone interviews: Interviews arranged by telephone rather than personal appearances, allowing the author to garner national radio exposure without traveling to every market.

3. When the book is published, the author will make one-hour presentations in fourteen cities: Seattle, Portland, Sacramento, San Francisco, San Jose, Los Angeles, San Diego, New York, Boston, Washington, DC, Philadelphia, Chicago, Dallas and Austin.

He will spend two days in each city to allow time for radio and television interviews, a lunch seminar and an evening seminar. The Charles Schwab Company has expressed an interest in hosting some of the seminars. The author is also soliciting The Learning Annex and Computer User groups. These will be in addition to or combined with the Prodigy seminars.

The seminar
Using a laptop computer and a special LCD projector that projects the computer screen, the author is preparing an hour-long talk to entertain and inform, giving a broad overview of investing, leaving the details for book buyers to find in *Win Big: Think Small*. The debut of the speech will be in March at the Stanford Business School annual Alumni Investment Seminar. The author is the chairman of this event and will repeat the presentation in 1995.

Sales/distribution
Beside the normal channels, the author will seek sales in areas such as the hundreds of investment and computer clubs by sending a press kit to each. If the publisher is willing, key opinion-makers in investing, politics, business, computers and academia will receive the book and the press kit.

    Among the opinion-makers that the author knows are Richard Hoey, chief economist of the Dreyfus Group; Maria Ramirez of Ramirez Capital Consulting, often on CNBC with analysis on the stock market; Tom Peters; Walter Shorenstein, the largest landowner in San Francisco and an active member in the Democratic Party; Tom Guba, managing director of Smith, Barney who will recommend it to Sanford Weill, chairman of Primerica Corp.;

Tony Frank, former Postmaster General; and Brad Child, senior investment officer of the government of Singapore."

For most books that you want to sell to a big publisher, your promotion plan will be the most important part of your proposal in determining the editor, publisher and deal you receive for your book. This is your chance to present, with controlled enthusiasm, your promotion plan for your book.

Jay Conrad Levinson believes that trying to promote your book without a promotion plan is like a general marching his troops onto the field of battle and saying "Ready. Fire. Aim." The best way to reach your goal is to plan the best way to get there.

Make your ideas creative and effective, but assume that you will pay for them. As long as you don't give the impression of being on an ego trip, your eagerness to promote your book will be essential in interesting a major publisher in your proposal.

Use the word *promotion* as a subhead for this part of the proposal. Then list, in descending order of importance, all of the things you will do to promote your book. Use the following list as a guide in creating your promotion plan. The greater the competition your book will face, the stronger your promotion plan must be to prove that your book will succeed.

HOT TIP Look at your book as a marketing tool. It's an excellent door-opener, a calling card that will help you gain access to any person or organization in your field. Whether you send a book, a media kit, a letter or just a postcard with the cover printed on one side of it, the publication of your book is an excellent way to let every key person in your field know you exist.

With most how-to books aimed at a large audience, you can generate far more money from the talks your book generates and back-of-the-room sales, and perhaps an audio or video version of it, than you can from royalties.

GETTING READY TO WRITE YOUR PLAN

Every book is a book, but every book is also a unique combination of author, content, publisher, timing, price, design, format,

editor and competition inside and outside of the house. The three
basic resources you have are your publisher, your book and
yourself.

The following suggestions will provide a logical approach to
making the most of your book's resources:

• From the moment you decide to write your book, use your
imagination to think about ways your book can be promoted.
Promotion involves a way of thinking about how to make your
book successful. Cultivate the knack of thinking in a creative,
promotional, anything-is-possible way. Develop a promotion re-
flex. Look at every person, place, event, trend and institution
and ask yourself: How can I use this to promote me or my book?

• Understand the competition your book will face for people's time and money from other books, media and activities.

• Join writers' organizations and go to writers' conferences.
Ask your publishing networks on- and off-line to share the techniques they find effective and help you figure out how to apply
these ideas to your book.

• Have a promotion potluck. Invite writers and have a brain-
storming session on one another's books.

• Analyze the nature, size and location of the markets for
your book and how to reach them as effectively and inexpensively as possible.

YOUR PROMOTION PLAN
Make sure your promotion plan excites your professional networks before you share it with agents or editors. Here is a starter
set of ideas:

• **Invest in your future.** Most writers can't make a living writing, much less spend money promoting their books. But a few
lucky writers who are doctors or lawyers, have succeeded in
another business, have extra income or have a working spouse
are able to earmark part or all of their advances for promotion.

If you can invest in your campaign, start your plan like this:
"The author will match the publisher's consumer, out-of-pocket
promotion budget up to x dollars." Out-of-pocket means that,
just as you won't be paid for your time, the budget also doesn't
include your publisher's staff time. It may be possible for you to

be compensated for your investment if your book or sub-rights sales are large enough.

We've represented authors willing to spend $50,000 to promote their books. However, equally important to spending money is proving that you have devised an effective campaign for your book.

• **Hire a book publicist.** Book publicists are specialists found in publishing centers around the country, in *Literary Market Place (LMP)* or through your publishing network. *LMP* includes book media and the names of the organizations of book publicists in New York, Los Angeles and San Francisco. Check on a publicist's experience, competence and reliability before choosing one.

Let your publicist help you put together your plan. Mention who your publicist is, ideally, somone whose name will impress the publishers you want to buy your book.

• **Describe your media kit.** A media kit can include anything that you think will impress the media, including the following:

> A news release about your book.
> A list of questions that you will rehearse answers for, including a few that have nothing to do with your book but might intrigue media people.
> Your bio.
> A black-and-white glossy photo of you for print media and television shows if there's no photo of you elsewhere in the kit.
> Reviews and articles about you with the good parts underlined, to be added as they appear.
> A small, fun, cheap, eye-catching, easy-to-mail, imaginative symbol of your book, maybe something with your name and title printed on it that will set your kit off from all of the others that inundate the media.
> An audio- or videotape of you speaking or being interviewed that will impress the media.
> A pitch letter tying this material together and explaining why you and your book will make a good subject for an interview.
> A paper folder with two pockets to hold the contents of the kit. If printing special folders for the kit is too expensive,

arrange to have extra copies of the cover printed, and paste it on the front of the folder.

> ⚡ **HOT TIP** Your promotion plan is not about the past, it's about the future. Describe your promotional experience in your bio.

• **Give yourself a free national tour.** Surveys have found that people are more afraid of public speaking than dying. So best-selling author Jerry Seinfeld has observed: "That means at a funeral, you're better off in the coffin than giving the eulogy." But if you can get paid to speak, take your act on the road. Try to hire lecture agents who are also listed in *LMP* to help you.

If you will travel to present classes, seminars, workshops or talks based on the book at which you will sell the book or include the book in the cost of the event—in other words, if you will send yourself on tour when your book is published—list the cities you will go to, starting with the major markets. "When the book is published, the author will give lectures in the following x cities:. . . ."

Assume your publisher will not send you on a national tour unless it has invested heavily in your book. But if your publisher knows that you will be traveling around the country when the book is published, its publicity department may be willing to approach local media about interviews.

If you are already giving presentations, you know where you will be able to arrange them when your book is published. If not, don't worry. You don't have to know where you will speak in each city. Once your manuscript is accepted, you will have nine months to set up places to speak.

When you start out, you may have to invest in promotion, but promotion of your book will be an opportunity for you to *make* money. Between fees for talks and back-of-the-room sales, set a goal of at least breaking even, with the publicity you generate being a bonus.

Your ability to profit from speaking will grow over time. Set realistic goals for yourself and your book, and do what you must to achieve them.

• **Keep going.** If you can, write the following sentence next:

"The author will continue to make x presentations a year."

• **Sell books.** Assume that 25 percent of your listeners will buy a book. If you can sell five hundred or more copies a year, include a round number. Your publisher may want to include the number of books that you will buy in the contract, so don't exaggerate. Use the largest round number that you feel comfortable with.

> ⚡ **HOT TIP** Buy a lifetime supply of your own books to be sure that you always have them. Despite contractual obligations, publishers sometimes let books go out of print before authors have a chance to stock up on them.

• **List well-known writers, experts or celebrities whose names will give your book credibility and salability, who have agreed to give you cover quotes.**

Obtain commitments for cover quotes from well-known writers, experts, celebrities and opinion-makers whose names will give your book credibility and salability in fifty states two years from now. Since book buyers around the country won't recognize your name, try to provide your publisher with endorsements from people whose names they will recognize.

Ask yourself whose names on the cover of your book will help convince potential readers to buy it. Unfortunately, the better known people are, the more beseiged they are with requests. But commitments for quotes from the right people can be powerful ammunition.

Once you decide to write your book, meet likely prospects at events or write to them praising their work. You can write to authors care of their publishers. If you can, mention that you will be quoting them in your book. Include a postcard so they can check off whether they will look at your proposal.

Be creative and resourceful in approaching this challenge. For example, if you are writing about the environment, consider asking Robert Redford, as well as the head of the Sierra Club, for a quote.

• **List the connections you have in business, government, the media or your profession who will help you promote your book and**

what they will do. If you've appeared on shows and been invited back, mention it. Matthew Shear, the publisher of St. Martin's mass-market division, once said that the seven most important words in publishing are: "It's good to be back again, Oprah."

Over the years, we've sold books that authors had published and proved would sell. When we sold Rick Crandall's book *Marketing Your Services: For People Who Hate to Sell*, editors were impressed with the names he had on the cover of his book as well as the sheer quantity of testimonials he had collected for it. Note also the money-back guarantee that lessens the risk of buying the book. Here's what Rick's proposal said about his testimonials:

> "The three stars featured on the cover—Harvey Mackay, Ken Blanchard and Tom Peters—will stimulate impulse buyers in stores. They may be the biggest names in trade business books over the last ten years. The colors and size of the book were chosen so that it stands out on the shelf. And the 100 percent money-back guarantee is unusual, encouraging browsers to buy.
>
> The book also has strong testimonials from Jay Conrad Levinson, the biggest selling marketing author (*Guerrilla Marketing* and many sequels) and Don Peppers, the hottest name in technical marketing today (*The One to One Future: Building Relationships One Customer at a Time*).
>
> The book opens with twenty-four different testimonials from service providers in alphabetical order from accounting, advertising and architecture to stock brokerage, surveying and window washing. Following these are fifteen more testimonials from experts. More comments are coming in all the time, so a new edition will have even stronger testimonials."

- **Consider establishing a Web site that will provide worldwide, 24-hour-a-day exposure for your book, enabling you to:**

> post your cover and a chapter online to promote your book
> update your book the moment you have new information
> list your appearances
> set up links from search engines and other Web sites
> stay in touch with your readers
> sell your book or include a link to an online bookstore that will give you a commission on the sales your site generates.

- **If you plan to mail copies of the book to opinion-makers in your field, mention in round numbers how many copies you will mail and to what lists.** If you need the publisher to supply the copies, write: "If the publisher supplies the copies, the author will. . . ." The publisher may be willing to mail at least some of the copies if you supply the mailing list or give you the mailing costs.
- **Special-interest magazines may be willing to trade an ad for a story.** If you can get a commitment, mention the size and cost of the ad and circulation.
- **A P.O. or "per-order" ad is one for which the magazine supplies the space, the publisher provides the books and the fulfillment, and they split the profits.** What will impress publishers is your being able to write: "X magazine (include the circulation if impressive) will run full-page per-order ads (Value $x) as long as they continue to pull."
- **If you can place a column based on your book in a magazine or newspaper or even give it away in exchange for writing your bio so it sells your book and services, mention it.**
- **Ask teachers in your field if your book has adoption potential in schools. If it does, write: "If the publisher wishes, the author will write an x-page teacher's guide."**

In their proposal for *Power Tools*, Russell and Roger Allred locked onto the schools around the country giving courses on the subject to help assure themselves continuing national exposure:

> "After publication, the authors will:
>
> 1. Conduct seminars in the following thirty-five cities: [List of cities followed]. Most of these cities have universities with family business departments that sponsor seminars.
> 2. Continue to present forty seminars a year to family business departments at universities, chambers of commerce, small-business development centers and associations of accountants, consultants, attorneys and independent business owners.
> 3. Sell thirty books a seminar or twelve hundred copies a year.
> 4. Encourage the universities to stock the book as a resource for their family business departments and course syllabi.
> 5. Visit the major bookstores in cities where the seminars are held to encourage them to stock the book.
> 6. Produce a videotape of a *Power Tools* presentation for distribution with press releases and media kits.

7. Prepare and distribute press releases and media kits to include a video- and audiotape, bios, a book cover and a business reply card for a book.

8. Appear on business-related interview shows in cities where the seminars are held. The authors work with a media consultant who has access to the major television shows nationwide.

9. Conduct at least forty-five telephone interviews a year on radio shows in smaller markets.

10. Write articles on a continuing basis for *Family Business Magazine, Inc. Magazine, Entrepreneur* and *Independent Business Magazine* in exchange for a byline promoting *Power Tools*. The editor of *Family Business Magazine* has already promised an article on the book when it is published.

11. Conduct a forum interview over America Online and maintain an e-mail address on the Internet.

12. Obtain endorsements from Buck Owens, country singer and family business owner; Barbara Griswold, past-president of Executive Women International; Lou Barbich, past-president of the California Society of Certified Public Accountants and other respected family business advisors."

As you will see in the sample proposals at the end of the book, the longer and stronger your promotion plan is, the better. For *When Life Becomes Precious*, Elise NeeDell Babcock prepared two plans: one for when her book was published and a lifetime plan.

If your plan is longer than five pages, add a title page and place it either at the end of the proposal or in the left pocket of the folder in which you submit your proposal.

The time to approach an agent or editor about your book is when two things are in place:

1. Your networks tell you that, on a scale of one to ten, your proposal is a ten.

2. Your promotion plan is as long and strong as you can make it.

The need for promotion is perpetual. *Chicken Soup* authors Jack Canfield and Mark Victor Hansen advise writers to do five things every day to promote their books. Promoting your work may be the biggest challenge you face as a writer. Even with its inevitable pitfalls, it can be fun, exhilarating and profitable.

The quality of your promotion plan along with your ability and enthusiasm for getting behind your book without making it an ego trip will affect a publisher's decision to buy your book and the strength of its commitment to it. With the right plan, agents and editors will be eager to work with you.

Keep in mind, however, that this approach to promotion is based on what we found works for selling books to New York publishers. If these suggestions are too ambitious, at least for your first book, don't be concerned. You must align your efforts with your goals and do what *you* think will be best for you and your book.

But enough about your book. Now it's time to check on your competition.

Chapter Five

COMPETITIVE AND COMPLEMENTARY BOOKS, THE RESOURCES YOU NEED AND YOUR BIO

Habent sua fata libelli. (Books have their own destiny.)
—Terentianus Maurus, Roman author, A.D. 200

I f in your book hook, you can write that your book will be "the first book to . . . ," then you will face no competition, and you may proceed to the next section on complementary books.

However, we get calls about books from writers that will have competition, and one of the first questions I ask them is: "How many books are out there on the subject?" Sometimes, they have no idea what books will surround theirs on bookstore shelves, a response that proves they're not ready to approach an agent.

The more books that have already appeared on a subject, the larger the market has to be to justify another book on the subject. Your proposal must be able to overcome the competition.

At the same time, subjects like cats, the Civil War and saving or making money are timeless. Enterprising writers are always coming up with new ideas that become successful books. A fresh angle, a fresh face, a well-written book and enough promotional support will make any book sell.

Editors and their colleagues in sales and marketing will want you to do their market research for them. Once you've told them everything they need to know about your book, make use of the data you gathered when you researched competitive books to ease their fears about the competition.

You must convince publishers that:

1. You're an expert on the subject who knows about the competitive books.

2. You're being professional in the way you are approaching the project.
3. Your ability to assess the competition objectively means that you can judge your own book accurately.
4. You have used your knowledge to come up with a new slant that, despite the competition, justifies another book on the subject.
5. You know that editors need this information, if not for themselves, then for their colleagues. At large publishing houses, editors usually work on books in a range of subjects. But they also have specialties. There's usually at least one editor whose job is to take care of the house's sports books, while other editors are assigned to oversee the company's business, cooking, gardening books and other specific subjects.

Editors know about competitive books in their specialties, but not necessarily in all of the subjects that they edit books on. So even if they do know about competitive books, the other people on the editorial board who will help decide the fate of your proposal may not. You can influence their decision by providing the information they need.

Starting the description of each book on a new line, list competitive books in order of importance, supplying the:

- full title
- author
- publisher—omitting the location and the word *Inc.*
- year of publication
- number of pages
- format—hardcover, trade paperback, mass market
- cover price—without the .00: $25, not $25.00
- size of the book, if you are proposing an art or photography book.

This is the only place in your proposal where you can use sentence fragments with impunity. Avoid starting descriptions with *this book, it* or the title.

Instead, start with a verb and write two incomplete sentences: the first about what each book does, the second about what it fails to do. Keep these descriptions as short as possible.

End the list with a short statement of why your book will be different and better than your competition. You may use a list of reasons that begins: "(Title) will be better than the competition because it:"—then list the reasons, starting each with a verb. You may repeat what you wrote in your book hook but vary the wording.

If you're writing about dieting, parenting, relationships or psychological self-help, subjects about which there are hundreds of competitive books, write about only the most competitive half dozen or so, and provide just the information listed above about the next most important six or so others without describing them.

Keep this section as short as you can, no more than two pages. The proposal is about *your* book, not the competition. You must, however, convince editors that you have a knowledgeable, realistic perspective on what's out there and that you have done justice to the competition.

Writers don't usually have access to sales figures of books. However, if competitive or complementary books, which are explained below, have been best-sellers, mention it.

One number that measures a book's success that you can include for both kinds is the number of printings a book has gone through. That number is at the end of a row of numbers in descending order at the bottom of the copyright page. For example, this row of numbers—10 9 8 7 6—indicates a book is in its sixth printing.

If you have the ammunition to assert that your book will do even better than a previous successful book on the subject, you will impress publishers.

This is Rick Crandall's closing statement for his self-published book *Marketing Your Services: For People Who Hate to Sell*:

> "None of the competitive books are well distributed or visible, and all of them are dated. For instance, the Internet is not mentioned as a new marketing medium. Despite their shortcomings, several of the above have gone through many printings. So the niche is wide open in the stores.
>
> The strategy of *Marketing Your Services* is to give readers a book that is more streetwise, practical, action-oriented and state-of-the-art. In short, *Marketing Your Services: For People Who Hate to Sell*, is a better value."

Be factual, not self-serving when noting the deficiencies of competitive books. Assume the editor either has seen or knows about them, and may even have edited one of them. Will your book be more thorough, timely, beautiful, comprehensive or up-to-date than its predecessors? If you think your book will be better written or have a more commercial angle, your proposal must prove it.

Pamphlets, most self-published books, scholarly books from academic presses and professional books from specialized publishers, such as those for doctors, lawyers and real estate salespeople, don't count as competition because of their limited bookstore distribution, so don't include them. Don't include out-of-print titles or books that aren't aimed at the general public.

Editors will be concerned about the titles that will compete with your book. They will want to avoid bookseller and book-buyer resistance to your book because of similar books that have national distribution. You have to convince them that these books have not saturated the market for the subject.

Sam Horn's style was evident even in her section on competitive books in her proposal for *Tongue Fu! How to Deflect, Disarm, and Defuse Any Verbal Conflict*:

> "*Tongue Fu!* has only three major competitors:
>
> 1. *The Gentle Art of Verbal Self-Defense* (310 pages, Suzette Haden Elgin, Dorset Press, 1980). Published in eight languages with four follow-up books. The books contain useful information, yet they are a difficult read. Problems include small type and academic jargon.
>
> 2. *Verbal Judo: The Gentle Art of Persuasion* (222 pages, George J. Thompson, William Morrow, 1994). Claims to help readers control the outcome of every dispute in the home, classroom and board room. By a former policeman who created his methods for fellow officers. Focuses primarily on what to do when faced with volatile situations and potentially violent perpetrators.
>
> 3. *The Magic of Conflict: Turning a Life of Work Into a Work of Art* (254 pages, Thomas Crum, Touchstone, 1987). Shows how to apply the martial art of aikido to daily conflicts. Emphasizes the importance of being centered and outlines how to use this "New Age stress-reduction strategy" to turn struggle into success.

How is *Tongue Fu!* better and different?

Tongue Fu! will be fun to read. Its friendly, conversational style, thought-provoking Tongue Fu-isms, amusing anecdotes and motivational stories will make it a page-turner. *Tongue Fu!*'s brief, to-the-point chapters will be ideal for today's hurried reader. It will feature extensive white space and a visually appealing layout so the material is easy to access, understand and remember.

Tongue Fu! will not waste time on theories or dry rhetoric. It will feature practical, real-life ideas and will teach readers exactly what to say and do when someone is being unfair or unkind. *Tongue Fu!* will appeal to people of all ages and levels of experience. A variety of personal and professional examples will make the material relevant for readers whether they're secretaries or supervisors, parents or partners in a law firm. The techniques and concepts are timeless. *Tongue Fu!* will continue to sell for years to come."

Agents' and editors' opinions vary on whether to include information on competitive books. Even if your agent doesn't want you to include it, you must know the information so you can improve on the competition and be prepared to discuss the competition if an agent or editor asks you about it.

HOT TIP If all of the competitive books on the subject you're writing about were published by small or university presses, it may suggest that unless you can supply strong enough ammunition, your subject may not be commercial enough or is too far ahead of its time for a large house.

COMPLEMENTARY BOOKS

Even if no competitive books exist on your topic, keep in mind that every book will have complementary books. The success of books on the same subject that won't compete with yours will convince editors of its market value. If the books aren't well known, indicate what they cover. Give the title, author, publisher and year for six books or less.

If you are preparing your proposal for a specific publisher, be sure to mention books on its list that complement yours. Close with a statement on how the existence of these books proves the salability of yours.

This is the end of your overview, the first part of your introduction. By now, you have convinced an editor that you have a publishable idea and a promotion plan that will help make your book a success.

In the last two parts of your introduction, you will prove that your idea is practical and you have the experience and ability to write your book.

HOT TIP You have only one chance to lose your credibility as a writer or as an authority on your subject. One error, in style or content, and everything you write will be suspect. Try to make your facts and your prose impeccable.

Every word you write is either helping or hurting your chances of selling your proposal. Whether you aspire to write in the concise style of Ernest Hemingway or the exclamatory style of Tom Wolfe, become sensitive to every word you write. If anything isn't pulling its weight, improve it or remove it. Don't waste an editor's time. Make every word count.

RESOURCES NEEDED TO COMPLETE YOUR BOOK

Once you have completed the thirteen parts of the overview and proved you have a salable idea, it's time to prove that you have made a realistic assessment of the resources you need to complete your book, including the most important resource of all: you.

On the next new page entitled "Resources Needed to Complete the Book," describe the out-of-pocket expenses, starting with the largest, that will affect the size of the advance you need to finish your book.

Your largest expense may be travel. If you write that you need a certain sum for a trip, a publisher may offer that sum. Be specific about where you're going and how long you'll be there. For example: "Researching the book will require a two-week trip to New York." If the reason you're going isn't obvious, explain it.

Include round but specific figures for artwork, photography, an introduction, online time and permissions to use quotes or illustrations. Give the total for each kind of expense, not an item-by-item breakdown: "The book's photography budget will be $500."

Don't mention small items like the cost of office supplies, but if an expense like long-distance phone calls or a combination of expenses will run $500 or more, include the cost.

If you are not planning to type the book yourself, include the cost for having the manuscript keyboarded.

If you will use a freelance editor to help you write the book, indicate how much it will cost.

If you have more than three expenses, list them in column form with the type of expense on the left, the cost on the right and the total at the bottom of the list. For example:

Completion of the book will require the following expenses:

Permissions	$1,000
Fifteen photographs	650
Telephone calls	500
Typing	750
Total:	$2,900

Usually, the author pays for the expenses involved in researching and writing a book, including the permissions costs, and the publisher takes it from there. Publishers may, however, provide a separate advance for large expenses, and if they want a book badly enough, will pay for part or all of the expenses.

AAR members Susan Ann Protter and Sheree Bykofsky are among the agents who think that, except for a permissions budget, it's easier to negotiate for expenses if the resource list does not include dollar figures. Your agent may even prefer to omit resources entirely.

Because expenses will become part of the negotiation for the book, researching them in advance will save time later and adds to your authority as a professional by showing you've thought the project through and know the expenses that will be involved in writing it.

PERMISSIONS

To excerpt copyrighted material in your book—a passage, a page, a chapter, a short story or an illustration—you may need to obtain permission. Relatively short excerpts from copyrighted material may be considered "fair use," that is, they may be used without permission of the copyright holder. Publishers vary in how they approach permissions and the doctrine of fair use.

To establish the cost of permissions to use quotes and illustrations from books, look up the publishers in *Literary Market Place*, and contact the rights-and-permissions person. For permissions on material not in books, contact the copyright holder. Syndicates and magazines have flat rates they charge for permissions.

You usually will not be able to obtain an exact price until you know the publisher, format, price and first printing of your book. Nonetheless, try to get a price range for what they charge for similar permissions and use the midpoint for your estimate. If for example, they charge between $100 and $300, use $200 as your estimate.

Ask about the price for the United States including its territories, dependencies and military bases; Canada; the Phillipines; and nonexclusive rights throughout the rest of the world except for the British Commonwealth. This is the basic grant of rights your publisher will expect to buy.

In addition to the cost of these rights, copyright holders will want either a flat fee for world rights or will charge a fee for each country the book is sold to. Depending on who retains foreign rights, you or your publisher can arrange for permissions for an English edition and translations when it becomes necessary.

If you're doing an anthology, or if obtaining the right to use copyrighted material is essential to writing the book, or if you expect the cost of permissions to run more than $1,000, find out as much as you can about permissions for your proposal.

Make sure, if you can, that the copyright holder will let you use the material, and that even if you can't determine it precisely, the cost won't be prohibitive. Learning everything you can now may prevent you from proposing quotes or illustrations you can't obtain or can't afford.

If you're just using a few short quotes, it may qualify as fair use. If you must obtain permission, mention that completing the book will require permissions costs for x quotes or illustrations. If you are willing to pay for permissions and write them off as a business expense, write that "the author will pay for the cost of permissions."

Permissions costs may be a bargaining chip in negotiating your contract. If you're in the fortunate position of having more than one publisher bidding for your book, a publisher may be willing to pay for part or all of the permissions, give you a separate advance for them or even handle the paperwork on them. It is to your advantage to provide a ballpark figure for the cost.

Publishers vary in what they like to see in a permissions form. So after your book is sold, ask your editor for a copy of a permissions letter you can photocopy.

PACKAGING YOUR BOOK

If you're proposing an illustrated book and you want to package it—that is, provide the publisher with a disk ready for the printer or bound books—include the costs involved and your experience as a packager along with the publishing experience of your colleagues.

Suggest packaging only if you have experience in the field or are working with an experienced packager. Also, offer it as an option, unless you will only sell your book if you can package it. The publisher may prefer to take care of the editing, design and production.

DRAWING UP A PERSONAL BUDGET

In addition to making a list of out-of-pocket expenses for writing your book, make up a complete budget of your personal expenses. Keep in mind that publishers may regard an advance as a sum of money enabling a writer to meet expenses involved in writing a book. You must also factor in how you will pay the rent.

You need enough money so you can devote all of your time to completing your book, and editors know that the smaller the advance, the more time it may take you to turn in your manuscript.

TIMING YOURSELF

The time it takes you to research and write the proposal, and especially the sample chapters, will give you a reasonably reliable

> ⚡ **HOT TIP** Unless your book will be complicated to research or is large in scope, don't explain how you will write it. Let your proposal prove that you know what you're doing. If an agent or editor is working with another writer on a similar project, valuable information may wind up in a competitor's hands. If editors have questions about your research techniques, they'll ask.
>
> Two exceptions: If your book requires access to celebrities or VIPs, your proposal must prove that you have it. If you're writing a biography, indicate your access to the person or to information about the person. If the subject is dead, note whether the bio will be authorized and whether the estate is giving you access to the person's papers.

basis to judge how long it will take you to write the rest of the book.

Also try this: Once you have finished your proposal, go through your outline chapter by chapter, and using the time you spent on the sample chapters as a criterion, guess how long it will take you to do each chapter, then add the results.

Publishers want to start recouping their investments as soon as possible. They also want their books well written. Unless your book is on a hot subject and must be completed quickly, don't commit yourself to writing fifty thousand words in two months. Editors will not believe you're going to do a professional job, and they may offer you less money because it will only take you two months to complete the book.

The time you allot should make sense in relation to your writing experience, the time it takes you to write the sample chapters and the book's subject and length.

After you decide how long writing the book will take, give yourself a month or two as a cushion to allow for unexpected problems that force you to veer off course. Six months, nine months and a year are common deadlines. Yours should be what you feel will enable you to produce your best work.

UPDATING YOUR BOOK
Publishers want to publish a book and have it sell forever without having to change it. They're reluctant to do books that have

to be updated every year, unless, like almanacs, consumer guides or tax guides, a large enough readership needs the information.

If your book holds the promise of continuing sales but will require updating, indicate how often you will do it: "The author will update the book every x years." Try to avoid including anything in the book that will become outdated before the revision. To be considered a revision, at least 10 percent of a book must be new information. The fewer the revisions, the easier it will be on the publisher and on you.

The good news about a new edition is that it is treated like a new book. It appears in the publisher's catalog, the reps resell it and you have another chance to promote it.

If the information on resources only runs a paragraph, add it to the end of the overview. The last sentence about resources is this: "The author will deliver manuscript x months after the receipt of the advance." If time is the only resource you need, then this is the only sentence you need.

If your editor thinks your sample chapters are usable as is, you're in good shape. However, if you feel that you need feedback as you write, ask your editor if you may send one or more chapters as you finish them.

This may be particularly helpful at the beginning of your relationship to make sure that you're both on the same wavelength. If speed is essential, work out the best mutually satisfactory arrangement you can for balancing speed and quality and delivering the manuscript in pieces.

If you already have a partial or complete manuscript, the last sentence on resources should read: "X chapters of the book are finished in draft form, and the rest of the book will be completed x months after receipt of the advance" or "The manuscript is complete in draft form."

The trade-offs: The more of your manuscript that is finished, the less editors may offer for it because you will need less time to finish it. However, it's to your mutual advantage for your book to be published as soon as possible. The closer your manuscript is to completion, the sooner your book will hit the shelves.

Here are the resources Bill Yenne needed for *Hidden Treasure: Where to Find It. How to Get It*:

"Resources need to complete the manuscript:

Travel	$7,500
(to various concentrations of	
treasure sites and lost mines	
in the West):	
Equipment for field work:	2,500
Charts and maps:	1,500
Photos:	1,500
Total:	$13,000

The manuscript will be delivered one year
after receipt of the advance."

CHIN UP: SURVIVING THE EXERCISE

Sometimes unpublished writers must feel like the guy in the cartoon who walks into a bookstore and asks the clerk for a book on suicide, and the clerk says, "Why don't you try self-help?"

It may sound like you have to know everything about your book before you have fully researched it. What you have to do is convince editors that you know your subject, your idea won't require an unreasonable amount of time or expenses, you're giving them an opportunity to latch on to a winner and you will do a superb job writing it.

Editors understand that you are presenting the book only on the basis of what you know now. Once the project is sold, you and the editor will have an identical interest in producing the best possible book, and you will be free to improve on what you propose in any way that you and the editor agree will help the book. But a well-thought-out proposal may save you grief later by ensuring that you are writing the same book the editor is buying.

You don't have to be an expert on the subject when you begin researching it. Starting a proposal with just an open mind and a passionate, insatiable curiosity is better than setting out with misconceptions or prejudices. Another joy of the writing life is the opportunity to learn new things that enable you to grow both as a person and as a professional.

After you've finished the proposal, you will probably know more about the subject than an agent or editor. Your research will elevate you toward the status of an expert. Let the bio that follows prove you're a pro.

ABOUT THE AUTHOR

What really turns me on is that the author has in some way been preparing all of his or her life to write this book. There is a tremendous commitment on the author's part to this work. That commitment will evoke a mirroring commitment in me. That's publishing at its best.

—Toni Burbank, executive editor, Bantam Books in *Book Editors Talk to Writers*

The last part of the introduction is called "about the author." Start on a new page, and describe in descending order of relevance and importance everything about you that will prove you can write and promote your book. Start with your connection to the subject.

You may have a lot to be modest about, but avoid the extremes of false humility or hype. In *Book Editors Talk to Writers*, Simon & Schuster senior editor Rebecca Saletan notes that "in literary nonfiction or memoirs—books that are more like fiction—credentials are less important." On the other hand, the more ambitious your book is, the more your bio has to prove that you are up to the challenge.

Include every facet of your personal and professional experience that adds luster to you as a person and a writer: published work, publicity experience, jobs, years of research, education, awards, travel, hobbies, special skills, memberships, especially if you served as an officer in the organization. If your qualifications are unique and you didn't mention them in your overview, now's the time.

If you have had a book published, give the title, publisher and year. Indicate book and subsidiary-rights sales if they are substantial. Unless you've received raves in major periodicals, editors won't take the time to read complete reviews, so extract up to a page of favorable quotes. If the editor is not likely to be familiar with the source of the quote, describe the periodical and include the circulation if it's impressive.

If your book was blessed with a half page or more of quotes, type them in descending order of importance on a separate page with the heading: "From the Reviews of (title)." If your book did receive outstanding reviews in important magazines or newspapers, underline the good parts and enclose the review after the proposal or in the left pocket of the heavy paper folder in which you submit your proposal.

Name the periodicals in which your work has appeared, the number of years you've been writing or researching the subject, the number of articles you've had published, and the range of subjects you've written about if you think these figures will impress editors. If you've written articles about the subject of the book, specify when and for whom. If you have received letters about you or your book that will impress editors, include them.

Vary your sentence structure to avoid starting too many paragraphs with your name. Otherwise, your bio will read like a list.

Dennis Hauck's bio in his proposal for *The Emerald Tablet: Message for the Millenium* proves that he has the credentials and speaking and media experience that large publishers want.

> "Dennis William Hauck is an internationally recognized authority on the paranormal. A respected consultant and investigator for several national organizations, he remains at the forefront of modern research into unexplained phenomena. He has personally experienced a variety of paranormal manifestations and has interviewed hundreds of witnesses to events ranging from apparitions to UFOs.
>
> A founding editor of the *MUFON UFO Journal*, Hauck was editor for six monthly newsstand magazines (*ESP, Phenomena, Sea Monsters, Ancient Astronauts, UFOlogy* and *Official UFO*).
>
> For several years, he wrote a weekly syndicated column about strange happenings and has written dozens of articles for magazines and scholarly journals. Hauck lectures extensively about Fortean phenomena and has appeared as a featured speaker at a dozen international conferences. He is one of the leading advocates of treating all paranormal experiences as part of a larger phenomenon that parapsychologists call 'exceptional human experience.'
>
> Hauck has been interviewed on nearly three hundred radio programs, as well as numerous television talk shows. He was featured in William Shatner's *Mysteries of the Gods* (Hemisphere Pictures, 1976) and has consulted on several motion pictures, including *Close Encounters of the Third Kind* (Columbia Pictures, 1977). He is a paid consultant for Hollywood production companies working on three TV-movies based on true-life ghost stories. Hauck also works with television shows such as *Sightings, Encounters, Hidden Lives,* and *The Other Side.*
>
> He attended Indiana University and pursued his graduate studies at the University of Vienna in Austria. Today he works as a full-time

freelance author/lecturer, while serving as western regional director for the Mutual UFO Network and California director for the Ghost Research Society. He is also an active member of the American Society for Psychical Research and conducts scientific investigations into claims of paranormal activity.

Hauck translated a series of medieval German alchemical manuscripts, which led to this proposal. Hauck is listed in current editions of *Who's Who in California, The Dictionary of International Biography* and *The International Authors and Writers Who's Who.*"

HOT TIP Avoid using a resume instead of a biography. Resumes are too formal and contain information editors don't need. You may be applying for work, but you're not applying for a job. If you are an artist or professor, and you think your resume is also necessary to prove your qualifications, make it part of the appendix in the left pocket of the folder that you submit your proposal in. Make your bio a clear, concise description of your life and work. If you are writing a humor book, be funny if you can.

O'Connor's Rule of Infectious Enthusiasm

It's up to you to convey inordinate enthusiasm for your book to an editor—so much so that the editor becomes "infected" with your enthusiasm . . . and then your editor is able to convey genuine enthusiasm to editorial peers and marketing people. If they, too, become infected, they will share that enthusiasm with copywriters, sales reps, artists . . . on and on throughout the ranks of the entire house . . . ultimately infecting the retail and wholesale buyers with enthusiasm sufficient to buy your book. IT WORKS!

—from Richard F.X. O'Connor's *How to Market You and Your Book: The Ultimate Insider's Guide to Get Your Book Published With Maximum Sales*

The first five lines of the bio by Ted Allrich (how's that for a salable name!) provide all the credibility he needs to write *The Online Investor.*

"A professional investment advisor registered with the SEC, Ted Allrich is a graduate of the Stanford University Master of Business

Administration program. He launched his own advisory firm in 1991 and manages more than $22 million for individuals, trusts and IRA accounts."

FIRST-PERSON BIOS

Write your bio in the third person as if you were writing a news release about yourself. Editors will appreciate your modesty, and it will read better than a page full of *I*'s.

However, the energy and commitment needed to write and promote a book are so great that your desire to write it must be strong enough to weather whatever vicissitudes fate has in store for you. So if you wish, use the first person to convey your sense of mission about your book at the end of your bio. But remember that unless you are using your experiences in your book, this is the only place in the proposal to use the word *I*.

Indicate the exposure you've had in the media, especially in connection with the subject of the book. Including impressive articles about yourself with the significant points underlined, particularly if they're also about the subject of your book, will prove the acceptance of you and your idea in the media.

List everything that you include with your proposal as appendices in the table of contents for your proposal. If you use more than one article, place them at the end of the proposal or in the left pocket of the folder.

The following bio proves that Francesca De Grandis brings immense authority to her book, and that what she writes about is an integral part of her personal as well as her professional life. An editor will also be impressed by her school and media savvy.

"Raised by a Sicilian witch, I learned that spirituality must be practical. That earthiness is a tenet of Goddess spirituality and is expressed in *Be a Goddess!*. Top that for a promise if you can!

I completed a rigorous and rare seven-year training with Victor Anderson, a Master of the Faerie Tradition, to become a Celtic shaman. That training was possible because I was adopted into Victor's family, which had kept the old ways intact. Few Wiccan traditions today have such lengthy, in-depth training. Mr. Anderson has called me 'one of the very few . . . who has shown understanding of the endangered mysteries of my people. . . .'

I earn my living as a witch: a remarkable feat since I am one of only five people in the United States to do so. My prosperity as a professional witch is all the more remarkable since I work mostly in San Francisco, where the market is glutted with psychics, including first-rate teachers like Starhawk and Luisa Teish. Yet I am a major teacher in the Bay Area, and religious leaders refer students to me.

In 1986 I established The Third Road in San Francisco for Goddess spirituality. Through the oral tradition—my classes and counseling—my teaching has been successful for more than a decade. My national and international work has also been successful. I taught my tradition in England for six months in 1992.

When a National Public Radio program in which I was featured was marketed as an audiotape, its review in *The Whole Earth Review* mentioned my name along with Z. Budapest and Starhawk. My work on ABC's San Francisco affiliate KGO radio, where I hosted an occult special, also helps prove the marketability of my approach to shamanism. I was a regular guest on the old KSFO, am a regular guest on KPIX, San Francisco's CBS television affiliate, and I have shared my magic on Voice of America. Z. Budapest called me 'a real musical talent . . . haunting.' And Starhawk called my thesis for the New College of California 'a personal and magical journey by a witch who knows her stuff.' I am the subject of a documentary aired on PBS.

I led workshops at the 1995 Massachusetts Rites of Spring and the 1995 Middletown, California, Ancient Ways Festival and led one of the main events at the 1996 Wiccan Conference in San Jose as well as one of the larger events at the Covenant of the Goddess's 1996 national conference.

An interview with me appears in *People of the Earth: The New Pagans Speak Out* by Ellen Evert Hopman and Lawrence Bond (Inner Traditions-Destiny Books, 1995). Other recent presentations include an interfaith ritual at the six thousand-member Chicago Parliament of World Religions, a storytelling performance at the long-established Intersection for the Arts in San Francisco and a lecture on Mysticism and Art at the San Francisco Art Institute. The online magazine *Witches' Brew* published a feature article on me in late 1996."

Avoid the words *currently* or *at present*. Just use the present tense.

If you have media experience, describe it. If you have a tape of an interview, send it to publishers with the proposal. Wait until an agent requests a tape before sending it. Whether or not you've had experience doing interviews, express your eagerness to do publicity. Avoid the words *willing* or *available*. Publishers assume you are. They're looking for the word *will*.

Point out your background as a speaker or teacher, or experience with promotion that will enable you to help your publisher push your opus.

If you have a brochure about your business that will impress editors, include them as appendices in the left pocket of the folder.

If you plan to write books on other subjects, list up to three of them in the order of their commercial potential, and indicate how long it will take you to write each one. As noted earlier, agents and publishers are eager to discover authors who can be counted on to turn out a book or more a year.

Limit your description to one line of copy. Every idea that editors like is another reason for them to work with you. You might wind up selling a book you're thinking of writing instead of the one you propose.

If you have a family, mention it along with where you live.

Letting your personality shine through in your bio without being intrusive is fine, especially if it will help sell the proposal or promote the book. However, cute is out, as are humor (unless you're writing a humor book), far-out approaches to telling your life story and sympathy for the editor, as in "I know that many books pass your desk, but. . . ."

 HOT TIP Your bio may be the easiest part of your proposal to write so you may decide to write it first.

Picture yourself

Affix a 5″ × 7″ or an 8″ × 10″ black-and-white photo of yourself at the bottom of the page or centered on a blank, unnumbered page after your bio. Your photo can help sell you as a professional, promotable author. Ideally, it should relate to the subject of the book. If you are writing a book about fly fishing, aim for a photo of you standing in your waders casting into a stream.

If you are not able to use your computer to print your photograph, a photocopy will be acceptable for a multiple submission. A photo in a story about you that makes you look "mediagenic" will suffice.

If you are sharing authorship with a writer, photographer, or illustrator, include a bio and a photo of each of you on a separate page.

IF YOUR BOOK IS COMPLETE

If you have a complete manuscript, read chapter nine to see if you should be submitting all of it. You don't have to prepare anything described beyond this point if you're submitting a complete manuscript, but you should include information on future expenses such as artwork and permissions in your cover letter. If you're submitting a self-published or out-of-print book, please see chapter twelve on how to submit it.

It may take you a lot of time and effort to get to this point in your proposal, yet the three parts of your overview may add up to less than ten pages. The next challenge is to prove that you can use the raw data you've gathered to produce a book that's worth putting between covers. On to the outline!

⚡ HOT TIP Your proposal is a writing tool that enables agents, editors and you to see a map of the territory that your book will explore.

However, your proposal is primarily a selling tool, a business plan in which you want publishers to invest. No matter how juicy the subject is and how well you write about it, if you can't convince a publisher to buy your book, it won't make any difference.

So after the subject hook and the book hook, feel free to arrange the parts of your overview in whatever order will best sell your proposal.

PART TWO

Baring the Bones and Sampling the Steak

Chapter Six

THE OUTLINE

The Golden Rule of writing an outline:
Don't write about the subject; write about the chapter.

I t's not a book, it's an article." Almost every new agent has heard this fatal complaint from an editor rejecting a proposal. The following pages will prevent your proposal from suffering this fate.

After you have marshaled the ammunition for your book, the next challenge is to assure an agent and editor that you have researched the subject well enough to prove that there's more than enough information in the idea to fill a book.

The outline of your book is the bones, the pieces of information that fit together to form a harmonious structure that enables the editor and you to envision the finished manuscript.

Your outline must convince publishing professionals that you have come up with the most effective way to present your information, and it must arouse them to read the sample chapters that follow.

Writing your outline also gives you the opportunity to prove three things to yourself as well as to an editor:

1. The quantity and quality of information you uncover justifies at least one juicy book on the subject.
2. The book will be commercial enough to justify your efforts.
3. You will enjoy writing it.

YOUR LIST OF CHAPTERS

The first page of your outline is a double-spaced list of chapters. The best time for editors to see the list is just before they start to read your outline.

At the top of the first page, type and center these two lines:

The Outline
List of Chapters

Along the left margin, type the number of the chapter, then the title, and flush right, the number of the page the outline begins on:

Chapter 1: (Title and Subtitle)   11

Give each chapter a title as clear, compact and compelling as the title of your book. If you wish, give chapters catchy or intriguing titles, then use subtitles to tell and sell: Tell readers what the chapter is about and give them a compelling reason to read it. If your subtitle will spill over to the next line, type the title and subtitle on separate lines.

Make your list of titles flow naturally and create a sense of continuity in time, tone and structure. Try to make your list of chapter titles, like the menu at your favorite restaurant, whet the editor's appetite for the outline that follows.

Try to make the title of every chapter read like the headline of an ad that compels people to read the copy that follows. Make your titles humorous if you're writing a humor book.

Consider giving your book a superstructure by dividing it into parts. Give each part a title. If it will help your readers, plan to write a page or less to introduce each part. Outline in about a paragraph what the introduction to each part will contain. Deciding to divide your book into parts and creating chapter titles are two more opportunities for you to use successful books as guides.

Type chapter titles and subtitles in upper and lower case. At the bottom of your list, add the word *Appendix* and the page on which you will describe it, if you find it necessary to explain what your appendix will contain.

The chapter titles for Steve Capellini's *The Royal Treatment: Taking Home the Secret of the World's Greatest Spas* capture the engaging, down-to-earth tone with which he wrote the book. The range of topics makes the book look comprehensive. Note the superstructure Steve gives the book by dividing the chapters into two parts.

Check the table-of-contents pages of successful books for the style of chapter titles that you want to emulate.

What? No outline?

Certain kinds of books such as cartoon books or picture books may not lend themselves to being outlined. But editors will expect a book to have a unifying theme and structure.

When I wrote the proposal for *Painted Ladies*, instead of just proposing a book of photographs of houses, I gave the book a structure by dividing it into four sections covering parts of the city. Later, we added another element to the structure of the book by arranging the photographs in the order of an architectural tour.

The point is to impose some kind of form on your idea. If the best way to structure your book is not already clear, reading the outline instructions may stimulate ideas.

TWO APPROACHES TO SIMPLE OUTLINES

Here are two simplified outlines:

1. If your book will consist of a series of chapters, each with the same structure and presenting the same kind of information, you don't have to prepare the in-depth outline called for below. Just list the chapters and then list what each will contain. This simplified outline can follow the book hook in the overview. For example, if you were going to write a guide to Europe's ten greatest cities, you would list, in order, the cities the book will cover then, also in order, list the resources of the cities that the book will cover.

2. If you are planning a compilation of information such as an almanac, a dictionary or an encyclopedia, list in order the topics the book will include. For Leonard Roy Frank's *The Random House Quotationary*, he listed the 637 categories of quotations he planned to include.

The following is the first page of Leonard's list:

Category Index

A	ACTING/ACTORS
ABILITY (= category)	ACTION
Includes—Skill	ACTION & TALK
Talent	ACTION & THOUGHT
ABSTINENCE	adjustment
Includes—Asceticism	See Conformity
Self-Denial	ADVERSITY
accident	ADVERTISING/PUBLIC
See Chance	RELATIONS

Includes—Promotion
Publicity
ADVERTISING: COPY &
SLOGANS
ADVICE
African-Americans
See Racism
AGE
AGE & YOUTH
AGNOSTICISM
agriculture
See Farming/Gardening
ALCOHOL
ALIENATION
ALLIANCES/TREATIES
ambassadors
See Diplomats
AMBITION
AMERICA: AMERICAN VIEWS
AMERICA: NON-AMERICAN
VIEWS
ANARCHISM
ANGER
ANIMALS
answers
See Questions & Answers
anti-feminism
See Feminism, Anti-
anti-semitism
See Jews: Anti-Semitism
ANXIETY
Includes—Worry
aphorisms
See Sayings
APPEARANCES
APPEASEMENT
APPLAUSE
ARCHITECTURE
ARGUMENT/DEBATE
ARISTOCRACY
Includes—Nobility

ARMIES/NAVIES
Includes—Militarism
The Military
arrogance
See Egotism
ART
asceticism
See Abstinence
ATHEISM
AUTHORITY
avarice
See Greed
awe
See Wonder/Awe
B
bad
See Evil
BANKS/BANKERS
BEAUTY
BEGINNINGS & ENDINGS
BELIEF
benefits
See Gifts
The Bible
See Scriptures
big business
See Corporations
bigotry
See Prejudice/Bigotry;
Racism
BLAME
blunders
See Mistakes
BODY
BOLDNESS
BOOKS/READING
BORES
BRAIN
BRAINWASHING
BURDENS
BUREAUCRACY

DISCOVERING WHAT YOUR BOOK WANTS TO BE

Michelangelo believed that his statues were waiting for him inside the blocks of marble he carved with hammer and chisel. Imagine that you are a sculptor and that your idea is presented as an enormous block of marble. Inside it is a magnificent edifice, the perfect embodiment of your idea.

Your job is to use your vision and skills to construct a sturdy foundation and chip away the superfluous until only a beautiful, organic structure remains in which form and function are inseparable.

Your outline is not a showcase for you to dazzle editors with your style, but the opportunity to show how well you can research, organize and outline your book. Editors will judge your introduction and outline on content, not style.

Even though your outline can't be a stylistic triumph, every word still counts. Providing a sound structure for the individual chapters and for the book as a whole demonstrates a firm grasp of the subject and how best to translate it into book form.

A skimpy outline will have editors asking themselves: "How do I know this is a book and not just an article?" A thin outline also invites problems from the unexpected. By not thoroughly investigating what's involved in writing your book, you are more likely to encounter more books to read, places to go, people to interview, illustrations or permissions to obtain than you describe. So do enough research to write a solid outline. A thorough outline is the best way to prevent unpleasant surprises as you write your book.

With both their sample anecdote and their list of the chapter's other anecdotes, Peter and Susan Fenton did an excellent job of giving editors a provocative, humorous glimpse of what this chapter from *I Forgot to Wear Underwear on a Glass-Bottom Boat* will be like.

"Chapter Two

Love and Sex   18 Pages

The eight tales in this chapter prove there's more to love and romance than wine and roses. Secret-tellers share their most intimate confessions, such as the fitness pro who sees sex as an opportunity for an extra workout.

Sample Story
The Only Way We Can Get Ready for Romance Is to Do The Twist
For some people, it's flowers and a gourmet dinner in the best restaurant in town. For us, dancing The Twist unlocks the door to romance!

My husband and I are Baby Boomers who met as teens in high school. We did all the fun things kids did back in the sixties—sock hops, midnight movies and endless cruising.

Our absolute favorite activity, though, was dancing at parties. We'd turn the lights low and slow dance for hours. But one night our pals introduced us to a brand new sound—Chubby Checker's version of The Twist. It hooked us! We spent hours mastering the art of The Twist, even practicing in front of a full-length mirror to get our moves down. Our friends really admired our style.

It was during this time that we fell in love and made plans for marriage after our high school graduation.

We exchanged vows when we were both just nineteen. Then married life began for real: four babies all in a row, a husband who was establishing his own business and plenty of money worries.

Without wanting it to happen, passion took a back seat to the pressures of everyday life. Although we still adored each other, we somehow lost the sexual bond that keeps a man and a woman together.

That is, until the day we heard The Twist again—after twenty-five long years. A radio station was playing the song as we were driving home from the kids' track meet.

My heart suddenly skipped a beat. The music stirred up emotions that I thought had long since died. I glanced over at my husband and saw his eyes light up with love.

When we got home, we twisted our way to the bedroom—and the most wonderful night of passion we've ever known. Since then, whenever we want to set the mood for love, we turn the lights down low—and turn on with The Twist!

Other Secrets in this chapter:

Fitness Nut's Secret 'Intercourse Workout'
I Wear a Surgical Mask When I Make Love
I'm with 32-A: Boyfriend's Secret T-shirt Has Her Fuming
I Made My Hubby Lose Twenty-Five Pounds: Now Beer Bellies
    Turn Me On
Marriage Made Me a Hit With Men
My First Orgasm Sent Me to the Emergency Room
I Waited Sixty Years for the Girl of My Dreams: It Wasn't Worth
    It"

A ONE-SENTENCE OVERVIEW

To help an editor grasp the essence of a chapter quickly, consider beginning an outline with a one-sentence overview of the chapter. Here are three ways to do this:

1. This chapter . . .
2. The goal (aim, purpose, object) of this chapter is to . . .
3. This chapter is divided into (consists of) x parts.

The last alternative has the added virtue of telling the editor about the structure of the chapter. If you use this approach, you can write a paragraph about each of the parts, perhaps starting each with a catchy subhead.

Here are the first sentences of the outlines for two chapters in Michael Lillyquist's *Sunlight and Health: The Positive and Negative Effects of the Sun on You*, which suggest other ways of starting a chapter outline:

> "The second chapter serves as an introduction to the knowledge about the nature of sunlight and its effects.
>
> The final chapter addresses the advances civilization has made with the advent of artificial lighting as well as the problems encountered."

Outlining a chapter with a series of one-line topics set off with letters or numbers looks academic, raises questions a list can't answer, and doesn't explain enough about the chapter. So start each chapter outline on a new page, and describe the contents of the chapter: the instructions in a how-to book, the characters and events in a history or biography, the development of a book's thesis.

HOT TIP Aim for one line of outline for every page of manuscript that you envision. For a chapter with nineteen pages, aim for nineteen lines of outline—about one line of copy for one page of manuscript. For every twenty-five lines of manuscript, write one line of copy. This makes the length of your outline correspond to the length of your chapter. You will learn how to guesstimate the length of your chapters below.

A chapter outline may run from one paragraph to two pages or more, depending on

- the kind of book you're writing
- how much information you have

- how long the chapter will be
- whether you include an anecdote or an opening paragraph of your chapters
- whether you will include sample chapters with your proposal
- how long an outline your agent prefers.

For most books, however, a page or less of outline for each chapter is enough. As everywhere else in your proposal, use as few words as necessary. If you're not planning to include sample chapters, consider compensating for that by doubling the length of your outline.

Starting your chapter outlines with the strongest anecdote you have from each chapter will help make your chapter outlines enjoyable to read, give editors a feeling for the flavor of your chapters and excite them about your book.

Use anecdotes that run from a paragraph to a page at the most. Even if your outlines will have anecdotes, continue to aim for one line of outline for each page of manuscript.

> **HOT TIP** Establish literary goals for each chapter as well as your book: What effect do you want the chapter to have on your readers? How much humor do you want in a chapter? How many anecdotes? What emotions do you want your readers to feel? Will the anecdotes you plan to include have the desired effect?

Write the outline *your* book needs. If your book calls for chapter outlines of a half a page or less, type the outlines one after the other instead of putting each chapter on a separate page.

Outline every chapter, including those you submit as sample chapters, so an editor can see how the chapters flow into one another, how your manuscript will hang together and how a page of outline relates to a completed chapter.

If you want the book to start with an introduction about whatever you want readers to know before launching into the text, outline it just as you would a separate chapter. Since the introduction may be shorter than a chapter, the outline for it may also be shorter. In their haste to dive into the book, readers may skip the introduction, so write about the book, not the subject.

If your subject needs an introduction, make it the first or second chapter. Just as the beginning of your proposal has to hook the editor to the proposal, the first chapter of your book must hook your readers. If it doesn't, why would they continue? Would you? Depending on the kind of book you're writing, the first chapter may be short, but make it as enticing as possible.

Hal Bennett, the author, ace editor and ghostwriter with whom I wrote *How to Write With a Collaborator*, has observed that successful books sometimes start with an account of how the writer came to write the book. This connects the writers with their readers and convinces them to find out what the excitement is all about.

If you're writing a how-to book, consider starting the chapter with an anecdote about how someone has used the book's advice to solve a problem, or what readers' lives will be like after they learn the skill you are about to teach them.

OUTLINE STYLE: FORMAT AND LENGTH
Start the first double-spaced page of each outline like this:

Part X: Title
(on the first page of each part)
Chapter X

Title of the chapter   x Pages, x Photos
(Flush left)   (Flush right)

Chapters usually range from fourteen to thirty-four manuscript pages. Fewer than fourteen pages may seem slight, and once a chapter starts running longer than thirty-six pages, consider dividing it into two chapters. Let comparable books point you in the right direction.

On the other hand, if you can write with confidence that each chapter will be the same length or that your chapters will average x pages, make this point in the overview in the section on special features. Then you don't have to give page lengths in the outlines, and you can center the chapter titles.

INTEGRATING ILLUSTRATIONS INTO YOUR OUTLINE
When you mention a person, place, event, fact or instruction you plan to illustrate, add the word *photo, graph, map, drawing*

> ⚡ **HOT TIP** The number of lines of outline you write for your chapters won't usually end in in five or zero nor will the page count of your finished chapters. So avoid having all of your page counts end in "5" or "0." It's too easy to pick those numbers and it may sound like you are just picking the first number that leaps to mind instead of thinking through how long your chapters need to be.

or *chart* after it in parentheses. An alternative: Skip a line after the end of the outline, type the word *Illustrations*, then list them in paragraph form in the order they will appear and what kind of illustration each will be, if they will vary.

Editors know you are guessing, and you'll be free to make changes in what you propose. But editors want proposals that present a clear vision of every aspect of the book.

FIGURING OUT HOW LONG YOUR BOOK WILL BE

Remember that manuscript pages have ten words to a line, twenty-five lines to a page so they're about 250 words. Book pages, on the other hand, contain more words. When your manuscript becomes a book, the page count will be reduced by at least one-third. The number of pages and chapters in books you want to emulate will help you decide on the numbers for your book.

Add up the number of illustrations you envision in each chapter. Then add the number of pages in your chapters to the page count for the back matter that you included in your overview and you will obtain the figures you need for your book hook in your overview. Your agent may prefer to have only these totals in the proposal without including the numbers for each chapter.

USING YOUR SAMPLE CHAPTERS TO
FIND CHAPTER LENGTHS

Writing your sample chapters will give you a sense of the relationship between outline and manuscript. As you write the sample chapters, you will develop an understanding of how an outline corresponds to a finished chapter.

After you have written the sample chapters and completed

your outlines, go through the outlines paragraph by paragraph, and based on your experience of how the outlines evolved into sample chapters, estimate how many pages of manuscript each paragraph of the outlines will become. It will usually be clear whether a paragraph in the outline will turn into three, five, seven, ten or more pages. You'll get the knack of it as you do it.

FAST FIXES FOR FOUR PROBLEMS

Be as specific as your research allows you to be about your ideas, facts, people, statistics, dates, advice, instructions, incidents and anecdotes, but avoid the word *specific*. Instead of writing *several*, write *four techniques*. If you have space on the page, list them.

Because you are preparing your outline for agents or editors, avoid the word *you* as if you were talking to the reader. One exception is if you will include a list of suggestions for readers in the outline. Here's an example:

"This chapter explains ten suggestions for getting along well with agents:

1. Remember that your agent works for you, you don't work for your agent."

The word *you* makes sense here, because this suggestion will be used both in a chapter outline and in the book.

Put your quotes into context. Identify the sources of your quotes as I have done with the quotes at the beginning of this book's chapters. If the book, person or periodical is not well known, include additional information such as a date, place or circumstance, to place the quote in context. Likewise, if you mention a person or incident, include enough information so an editor understands what you're writing about and why. The outline for *The Mayor of Castro Street* in chapter eight does this well.

Avoid asking rhetorical questions. Questions editors can't answer don't help sell your proposal, so avoid questions altogether in your overview and outline. The purpose of the proposal is not to ask questions, but to answer every question an editor may have about you and your book. The only part of the proposal in which questions make sense is the sample material, in which you're free to address the reader.

Here's an outline from the first edition of my book that later became *Literary Agents: What They Do, How They Do It, and How to Find and Work With the Right One for You*:

"Chapter Twelve

Good Fences Make Good Neighbors
How to Handle Agency Agreements   19 Pages

This chapter starts by balancing the pros and cons of agency agreements. Then it covers eleven essential points that should appear in any agreement, as well as clauses for writers to avoid. Four representative agreements follow, including the author's which appears on the next two pages.

The discussion of agreements concludes that since no agreement can encompass every potential contingency, the most important basis for any agreement is the good faith of the people who sign it.

The next part of the chapter presents a separate Bill of Rights for authors and agents stating their responsibilities to each other whether or not the agents have an agreement.

The chapter ends by analyzing the causes for changing agents and the three-step procedure for doing it:

1. Try to find a mutually satisfactory solution to the problem.
2. If that is not possible, notify the agent in writing of the change.
3. Find another agent."

Now that you have an overview of preparing your outline, you are ready for the two keys to making your outline effective.

Chapter Seven

VERBS AND STRUCTURE: THE TWO KEYS TO WRITING YOUR OUTLINE

I'm looking for a sense that the author is capable of dealing with structure. I want the confidence that the author is capable of organizing the whole project and taking on a big thing like a book.
    —Simon & Schuster senior editor Rebecca Saletan
    in *Book Editors Talk to Writers*

If you simply summarize your chapters, the outline will read like an article or mini-book, and editors will reject your proposal, thinking that the idea doesn't have enough substance for a book.

GIVE EACH CHAPTER A STRUCTURE
Giving each chapter a structure makes your chapter outlines read like outlines instead of summaries.

You will find one of these three approaches effective:

1. Use a number in a title like *10 Steps to X*, a common device because it communicates immediately what the chapter will do for readers.

You can divide a chapter into parts that become the organization of the chapter (and your talk), and can also be mentioned in the title of the chapter. For example: "Four Reasons Why You Should Quit Smoking." Don't overuse this technique, or your book will read like a series of formulas.

2. Structure each chapter with a beginning, middle and end.

Indicate the structure by introducing each part of the chapter. Here are alternative openings for the successive parts of a chapter:

First, the chapter . . .
The first (opening) part (section, segment) of the chapter . . .

The chapter begins (starts, opens with) . . .
. . . starts (begins, opens) the chapter.
In the opening part (section, segment) of the chapter, . . .

Next comes (is) . . .
At this point in the chapter, . . .
The next (following, middle) part (segment, section) of the chapter . . .
The chapter then . . .
In the following (next, middle) section (part, segment) of the chapter, . . .
. . . follows (comes next).
The chapter's next (middle) section (segment) . . .

Finally, the chapter . . .
The last (final, closing, concluding) part of the chapter . . .
The rest of the chapter . . .
The chapter ends (concludes, closes) with . . .
. . . ends (concludes, completes) the chapter.
In the last (final, closing, concluding) part of the chapter, . . .
The chapter's conclusion . . .

Outlining your first book is a new skill that will take getting used to, but you will get the hang of it, and a thorough outline will help you even more than your publisher. Two quick tips: Write *the chapter*, not *this chapter*. Be creative in how you vary your wording.

3. Conceptualize the information in each of your chapters in the form of an image or symbol that captures the essence of the chapter in a unifying, memorable way and may provide the structure for the chapter.

Is it possible to visualize the material in your book or a chapter of it as a shape like a circle, or a pie, the slices of which constitute the substance of the chapter? Could the information be compared to a jewel, a plant, an activity, a machine, a person, a place, a period or event in history? Like an evocative title for a book, the right image can convey the tone and structure of a chapter.

For example, my book about literary agents has separate chapters about a terrible day and a terrific day in the life of an agent. Starting in the morning, I made up a composite of the horrible and wonderful things that have befallen our agency over the years.

The search for the proper structure for your chapters and your book is another example of how reading comparable books will start your creative juices flowing.

USING "OUTLINE" VERBS

Another way to make your outlines read like outlines is to use "outline" verbs that tell what the chapter does.

For instance, instead of writing a description of the Left Bank in Paris, write: "The next part of the chapter describes the Left Bank in Paris. . . ."

To give you a better feeling for outline verbs, here is an alphabetical potpourri of them culled from *Roget's II: The New Thesaurus*, a handy resource to check if you find yourself stuck for the right word. You don't have to read the list now, but keep it handy as you prepare your outline.

address	confirm	encourage
advance	confront	establish
advise	continue	evaluate
advocate	convince	examine
affirm	debunk	expand
agree	defend	explain
analyze	define	explore
appraise	deliver	expose
argue	demonstrate	express
assert	deplore	focus on
assess	describe	follow
attack	develop	forge
balance	discuss	form
blast	dispel	give (voice to)
blend	dissect	go (into, on, over,
broaden	distill	through)
build (on, up)	document	hammer
center (on, around)	dramatize	harmonize
challenge	elaborate	help
clarify	emphasize	identify
complete	enable	illuminate

illustrate	proceed (with, by)	stimulate
include	prod	strive
incorporate	prompt	suggest
integrate	propose	summarize
introduce	prove	supply
investigate	provide	surprise
join	puncture	tackle
judge	put (an end to,	take (advantage of,
justify	before, in	a look at, issue
lay out	perspective, into	with, place, up)
lead to	context)	talk
link	question	tease
list	raise	teem
lock horns	recommend	tell
look	recount	thrill
maintain	refute	tie (together, up)
mark	reject	uncover
marshal	relate	undertake
mention	remind	unearth
move on to	reply	unify
name	report	unmask
narrow	resolve	unravel
note	respond	unveil
offer	reveal	uphold
outline	review	urge
paint	say	use
pepper	scrutinize	venture
persuade	set (forth, up)	vindicate
pinpoint	shake up	voice
place (in	share	warn
perspective)	shift	wax
point out	show	weed out
portray	sort out	widen
prescribe	specify	work out
present	speculate	

To expand the list, try adding the prefixes *dis-*, *re-* or *un-*; see if the opposite of a verb fits, or if you can use it as a noun.

To keep your outlines from reading like a formula, avoid using the same verb twice in the same chapter or more than four times in the outline. If you use a verb more than once, vary its form. Vary verbs as much as accuracy allows.

You can use many of the verbs above in three ways:

the middle section of the chapter reveals . . .
begins by revealing . . .
begins with the revelation that . . .

You can use verbs that involve readers or characters:

The chapter opens by encouraging (warning) readers to . . .
The following section takes (leads) the reader to . . .
In the last part of the chapter, the reader learns (discovers, finds out, meets, sees) . . .

If you're writing about people, you are free to use verbs that describe their actions. In a biography, however, avoid a string of sentences beginning with *he* or *she*.

Avoid the passive voice. Wrong: The issue of drunk drivers is examined. Right: The chapter examines the issue of drunk drivers.

> ⚡ **HOT TIP** Since your book doesn't exist yet, write about it in the future tense, but write your outlines in the present tense. Your chapters don't exist yet either, but your outlines use many verbs, and they read better without all those *wills*.

Here are three steps to ease your way into writing outlines:

1. First list the bare bones of a chapter either on index cards, a sheet of paper or your computer.
2. Then add the topics that each part of a chapter covers.
3. Then flesh out each of the topics with connective tissue.

Barbara Geraghty opens this chapter outline from *Visionary Selling: Think Like a CEO to Sell to a CEO* with a short paragraph that establishes the rationale for the chapter:

"Chapter Nine

Building Credibility and Trust . . . Quickly   14 Pages
                                        1 List, 1 Cartoon

The purpose of this chapter is to provide tools and techniques for building credibility and trust in every encounter in the prospect's organization.

The chapter begins by exploring corporate team dynamics and the importance of being perceived as a competent and trustworthy ally by everyone who may have an influence on the decision to buy or use a product or service.

The next part of the chapter discusses the importance of preparation for sales success and customer satisfaction, acknowledging salespeople's tendencies to improvise with two humorous anecdotes and a cartoon. The vital importance of asking questions, listening intently and asking additional insightful questions to penetrate to a deeper level of need is presented.

Then the chapter cites three examples of top salespeople losing business because they didn't do their homework and began sales presentations without understanding the real needs and issues of everyone involved in the decision.

The chapter concludes by providing twelve ways to build credibility in the prospect's organization."

THE VALUE OF CONTINUITY

Maintain continuity within and between chapters so there is a natural, graceful flow of ideas, incidents and information.

If you're writing a narrative that unfolds over time, include enough dates so readers can understand the progression of events and can see how each chapter advances your story. One solution: If you can divide your book into periods of time, consider indicating the time period at the beginning of each chapter.

If you are writing about a person, historical period, issue, system or endeavor, the subject will have a past. Put its past into context by providing a historical perspective. By the end of the outline, an editor should have a clear sense of continuity in the subject's past, present and future.

This doesn't mean that you have to start at the beginning. Start with a powerhouse first chapter which hooks your readers with as much intensity as you can deliver. Then you can backtrack to fill in the missing pieces.

Besides placing your subject in the context of time, also establish its geographical context, its relevance, if any, to what is happening in the field elsewhere in the United States and the world. This will be an expansion of the perspective you gave the editor in the subject hook of your overview.

Your outline should be so teeming with ideas and facts that editors will easily be able to visualize the proposal expanded into a full-length manuscript and be delighted at the prospect.

HOOKS THAT KEEP YOUR READERS READING

Whether you're writing a how-to, biography, history book or a book about science, look for the hook. Start each chapter with the right hook—a quote, event, anecdote, statistic, idea, surprise or joke—to grab your readers' interest and draw them into the chapter. You can also use a chart, diagram or illustration that captures the essence of the chapter.

Try to end chapters with a hook, climax or a provocative hint about the next chapter to induce readers to turn the page. If you don't include the hook itself in the outline, describe it.

If you can, begin or end a chapter with something compelling that is also new. As you outline your book, if you are presenting a new idea or information and editors may not know that, mention it. The new elements in your book help justify its existence.

Opening quotes can draw readers into a chapter, but try to make them fresh, concise and enjoyable to read. Avoid Shakespeare, Plato, the Bible and familiar quotes.

If you come across an informative or entertaining quote or anecdote that captures the essence of the chapter, put it, along with the source, at the beginning of the outline, setting it off by indenting it. You can also use a short passage of dialogue from a biography or history book.

However, don't use something in your outline if it will appear in a sample chapter. Save it for the chapter.

Here is how Joanne Wilkens started the outline for the third chapter of her proposal for *Her Own Business: Success Secrets of Entrepreneurial Women.* Note how Joanne called attention to this being the first chapter of its kind:

> *"Enough! I'm tired of waiting. If they won't make me a president, I'll make myself a president.*
>
> —Jayne Townsend, Jayne Townsend and Associates, Ltd., a management consulting firm

The company I worked for was doing poorly. I watched the boss lose money and knew I could do it better.

—Carol Hayes, landscape architect

This chapter will be the first chapter on the subject to examine why women decide to go into business for themselves."

Joanne began a chapter called "No Money, No Credit, No Business" with a quote that is also an anecdote:

"My business was self-supporting when I started so I didn't need any loan. After three or four years, I wanted a $5,000 line of credit so I took my tax returns to the bank. You could see that I was making more money every year, but the loan officer treated me very shabbily. I never felt like such a nothing.

—Marian Lee, owner, import-export firm"

HEADS UP: USING SUBHEADS

Separating sections of text with subheads breaks up an endless procession of paragraphs. Subheads will also make your outline easier to read, and if they're clever, they will engage the reader's interest in what follows. Since subheads will be part of your manuscript, they can address the reader. A quick tip: Don't overuse them.

To provide unity and continuity in the outline, begin and end chapters with introductory and concluding remarks. For the same reason, books often require "bookend chapters," an opening chapter that tells readers what you want them to know before they begin learning what your book has to teach and a concluding chapter in which you may summarize the book, speculate on the future or inspire your readers to act on the book's ideas.

When it comes to outlining a book, different kinds of books create distinct challenges for writers. The next chapter will help you solve the problem of outlining different kinds of books.

Chapter Eight

QUICK FIXES FOR SIX KINDS OF BOOKS

I started writing sophomoric articles for the college paper. Luckily, I was a sophomore.
　　—Anne Lamott, *Bird by Bird*

Alas, you can't use being a sophomore as an excuse for a shaky outline. One of the many reasons why now is the best time ever for you to be a writer is that there are more subjects to write about than ever before.

There are also more ways for you to approach these subjects than ever: as a how-to, pro or con, serious or pop, traditional or alternative, multicultural, high-to-low income in the form of a biography, a history, a look ahead, an illustrated book, a serious, popular or consumer reference book, a gift book, a novelty book, a humor book, an expose, an issue book or an inspirational book. Your book may be published as a hardcover, a trade paperback, a mass-market book or, in time, all three.

However, different kinds of books present different challenges in writing outlines. Here are suggestions for outlining six kinds of books.

HOW-TO BOOKS

How-to books are staples in the book business. Publishers welcome fresh ideas that enable readers to lead better, richer lives. Successful how-tos present a new idea at the right time, or are written by an expert, celebrity or promotable personality. If a publisher's lucky, a how-to will have a strong idea, a strong personality and the right timing. People want to know, but they don't want to learn, so your job is to make learning as easy and enjoyable as possible for them.

How-to books use six techniques to present their material:

1. They have a down-to-earth, me-to-you tone. At their best, as in Anne Lamott's book about writing, *Bird by Bird*, the author has a distinctive, endearing, inspiring voice that helps keep readers turning the pages.
2. They include humorous anecdotes both to create a rapport with readers and to help make the book as enjoyable to read as it is informative.
3. They give readers something to do to keep them involved.
4. If they are teaching a skill, they present it in a clear, step-by-step way that is reflected in the book's title and the chapter titles.
5. They supplement the text with attractive illustrations.
6. They are visually appealing.

If you are writing an instructional book like an exercise book or a cookbook, start each outline by describing the chapter's introductory remarks and plan on including copy between exercises or recipes. Besides creating a rapport between you and your readers, it allows your personality to shine through, breaks up the instructional material and makes your book a pleasure to read.

BIOGRAPHIES

A biographer is a novelist under oath.
    —Leon Edel, author of *Ars Biographica*

Biographies present the temptation to summarize a chapter instead of outlining it. "First, she did this, then she did this, and then she did this, etc." But if your summaries and sample chapters are rich enough, your proposal will still work. Brief passages of dialogue that convey your chapters' emotional impact will enhance your summaries.

Here are two outlines: one written in the third person for a biography, the other written in first person for a memoir.

The following outline of the first chapter of Randy Shilts's proposal for *The Mayor of Castro Street: The Life and Times of Harvey Milk* shows that it is possible to outline a biography in the form recommended above. Note how Randy gave continuity to the chapters by including the time period of each chapter.

"Part I: The Years Without Hope
Chapter One

The Men Without Their Shirts   29 Pages
Time: 1930-Korean War   2 Photos

The chapter opens with the story of how police round up a teen-age Harvey Milk with other gay men cruising Central Park, marching them off to a paddy wagon for the crime of taking off their shirts in a gay section of Central Park.

The police march the group through a family section of the park where shirtless men are left unmolested. For the first time, Milk realizes there's something wrong in society's treatment of gays.

This opening symbolizes Milk's life as a homosexual growing up decades before the phrase "gay rights" was ever used, and it also indicates the social climate facing gays of that period. The chapter develops both of these themes.

On the personal side, this segment outlines Milk's early family life on Long Island and his college years in Albany. Many of Milk's personality traits are evident during these years: his lust for the lime-light, his stubborn dogmatism, his sense of humor and most signifi-cantly, his intense interest in politics.

Milk's ramblings in New York's gay milieu of the mid-forties and fifties offer an opportunity to capsulize the social and political status of gays at the time. The chapter also briefly touches on the homosex-ual emancipation movement in Germany, which thrived well into the 1920s.

After telling about an experience of four-year-old Harvey Milk, for example, the narrative shifts to Germany in the same year when, on "The Night of the Long Knives," Hitler wiped out Germany's gay subculture. That marked the beginning of the dictator's attempts to exterminate homosexuals.

The gay genocide, coupled with the Jewish holocaust, exerts a powerful influence on Milk's thinking. Through such historical di-gressions, the first chapter introduces the book's four levels [de-scribed earlier in the proposal].

This chapter ends when Milk, at the apex of a budding career in the Navy, is booted out of the service because of his homosexuality.

Photos: Milk at four on a pony, and in Navy uniform."

In the following page from her proposal for *Wild Child*, Linda

Ashcroft deftly blends writing a first-person outline with giving an appealing sense of the intimacy of her friendship with Jim Morrison:

"Chapter Seventeen

Hands Upon the Wheel   28 Pages

This chapter examines our feelings for each other. I feel that Jim only asked me to marry him to liberate me from my father's control. Since I have vowed to my mother I will not marry until I am eighteen, there seems no reason for Jim to marry me. I free him of any obligation. He tells me he came to Maine, not to save me, but to save himself from alcohol.

The next segment shows us feeling lighthearted again. We decorate a rented room with a Kandinsky poster he bought on his European tour and start a collection of quotes for the wall with one from Rimbaud about the coming equality of women as poets. I go to school by day and sneak out of my friend's house after everyone has gone to sleep. Worn to exhaustion, I fall asleep amid my notes for a history paper. While I sleep, Jim writes the paper for me. He wants to mount a protest when it only receives a B+.

The chapter moves on with Jim and my mother making amends. Never before has Jim truly forgiven anyone, but he loves my mother enough to try to understand she meant to do the right thing (in an incident described earlier) and forgives her. After dinner, the three of us sit around the table while Jim reads his poetry. My mother only knows Jim as a poet. I ask if he might make the same gesture to his own mother. He walks away without an answer.

The remainder of the chapter is devoted to the drive along Highway 9 from Saratoga to Santa Cruz, where Jim starts humming the music that, in the course of the evening, will become 'Roadhouse Blues.' While I take the winding two-lane highway without so much as a driving permit to my name, Jim slouches down, knees on the glove box, writing in my diary, 'Keep your eyes on the road/your hands upon the wheel. . . .' "

INTERVIEW BOOKS

If you plan to write the history of Los Angeles in the movies, the information you need is available. If you outline it well, an editor can easily assess the proposal.

Books based on interviews, however, present a problem. Predicting the value of future interviews is difficult, even if you provide an editor with a list of interview subjects. You can't guarantee you'll come away with a book's worth of publishable material. Predicting the length of your chapters is also more difficult.

Another publishing reality to mull over: Publishers' sales reps cover fifty states and want books of interest to book buyers in their territories. If an idea has national scope, the research for it should be nationwide.

If, for example, you're profiling successful entrepreneurs, you can't just cover those in your area. Aim for as much diversity in location, background, type of product and service, experience, attitude and lifestyle as you can in those you interview. Editors will expect the book to be comprehensive in presenting the range of the entrepreneurial experience. Include people from major cities, which are also major book markets, and all regions of the country. The regional variations you encounter will add depth to your book.

> **HOT TIP** Use the opportunity to travel to give talks and develop your network of authors, media people, booksellers and speaking venues.

Interviews in your area, perhaps supplemented by telephone interviews elsewhere, may suffice for the proposal. You naturally want to minimize your expenses on a proposal that might not sell. But indicate in your overview and outline that the manuscript will contain interviews from around the country.

A problem might arise later if your interviews don't yield the material you want and you need more time or money to obtain additional interviews. Plan your research carefully and give yourself a cushion.

Interviewing as many people as you can in your initial research in person, by phone or online will enrich your proposal, help teach you how to overcome problems and provide leads for other interviews. After published articles, the most convincing argument for publishing an interview book is a hefty portion— a third to a half—of the manuscript.

Writers with interview articles to their credit may be attracted by the notion of doing a book of interviews, thinking: "Hey, I'll find twenty people who need publicity, do ten ten-page interviews and I'll have a book." Well, editors aren't wild about collections of anything, including interviews, unless the interviews are wedded by a very salable idea, or are with celebrities or VIPs whom people want to know more about, or the interviewer is famous, or all three.

Editors would rather you take an idea and develop it for at least 50,000 words, structuring the book around ideas and using interview material to prove your points. For editors, that's what makes a book a book.

HUMOR BOOKS

After he received S. J. Perelman's first book, Groucho Marx said to the humorist, "From the moment I picked up your book until I laid it down, I was convulsed with laughter. Someday I intend reading it."

Unless you have a track record writing humor or experience as a stand-up comic, humor can be hard to sell with a proposal. It's difficult to prove that you can be funny for the length of a book, even a short one. So if you can't deliver all of the manuscript, try to submit at least a third of it to present a solid sampling of your sense of humor. If you're doing a cartoon book with captions, provide all of the captions, as many drawings as possible and a description of the remaining drawings.

EXPOSES

Controversy can sell books if it's the right subject at the right time with an author who can publicize the book in a way that catches the attention of the media and the public.

Silent Spring by Rachel Carson, *The American Way of Death* by Jessica Mitford, *Unsafe at Any Speed* by Ralph Nader, *All the President's Men* by Bob Woodward and Carl Bernstein and the amazing string of best-sellers by and about O.J. Simpson have proven it.

Nonetheless, people don't like to get depressed, and they sure don't want to pay for the privilege. That's why unless they're written by a promotable author and about a hot subject—Hollywood, politics, big business or some other juicy subject with built-in national interest—exposes in general don't sell well.

If your book will bring bad news, try to be prescriptive as well as descriptive. People don't want to buy problems, they want to buy solutions. They want to take a book like they take a magic pill. So develop a program for making the situation better. This will give your book a positive slant that will improve your title and your sales. *Claiming Your Share* (page 3) is an expose, but Michelle Saadi turned the idea into a public service.

ANTHOLOGIES

Anthologies also don't light up the cash registers. In the book trade, even the word *anthology* is deadly. Avoid the notion of a collection in the title, if possible. *Sisters of the Earth: Women's Words on Nature* sounds like an anthology, but the title is more appealing without the word.

If you're doing a treasury (a less academic, more selling word), start with a strong concept, make sure the selections are worth including, that they measure up well against each other and that the book will hold up over time. Try to make your selections flow naturally from one to the next. Splitting up the book into parts and chapters and writing an introduction for each section helps ensure this. Consider including brief bios of your contributors.

Getting permissions, covered earlier, can be a time-consuming problem because copyright holders may be abroad, may not respond to your inquiries, may charge you an exorbitant fee or refuse to quote a price until they know how your book will be published. Yet it's important that your proposal include as accurate an estimate as you can obtain.

A FINAL THOUGHT: LAYING THE FOUNDATION

Writers have told us that writing the outline was the hardest part of doing the proposal. However difficult creating an outline may seem, keep in mind that besides impressing the publisher, you're doing yourself a favor.

If this is your first book, you will feel far more confident about tackling it once you've finished a couple of chapters and are armed with a clear vision of the rest of your book. Indeed, doing your outline will enable you to pick the best sample chapters to write.

Hal Bennett believes that a well-written outline can make writing your book "almost as easy as painting by the numbers." After using the outline as a guide in researching your book, your outline becomes a map guiding you as you write.

Learning to write outlines is less painful than learning to ride a bicycle, but it will last you as long. Like typing, the skill of outlining a book will serve you well as long as you need it. Like the rest of your proposal, it's a test of your commitment to your book.

Your outline is the foundation of your book. A sturdy, cohesive foundation will help convince an editor to back your proposal. A thorough outline may also prevent your book from being rejected. If you deliver your manuscript on time, and it lives up to what your proposal promises, your editor will have no reason to reject it.

How exact a blueprint your outline is for the finished manuscript will depend on how well you write your outline, the need to explore new avenues of investigation, suggestions your editor may make and how cut-and-dried or open-ended the subject is.

> **HOT TIP** If you have specific concerns about any part of your proposal, including the structure, ask your networks about them when you send out your proposal for feedback. The more precise you are about the advice you need, the more helpful your readers will be. Friends may give you the worst advice with the best of intentions. You must trust your instincts.

Your book may change unexpectedly because of new ideas or information or an unpredictable turn of events. But properly done, the structure you create for your book will serve you well as a framework for writing a book you can be proud of.

Chapter Nine

THE SAMPLE CHAPTERS

Life is one audition after another.
　　—Written on a T-shirt seen by the author in San Francisco

WHY A SAMPLE IS NEEDED

Your sample chapters are your audition for the role of author. If your introduction is the sizzle and your outline is the bones, your samples chapters are the steak. They are the meat of your proposal, a tasty sample of what's to come. They must be so substantial and enjoyable to read that editors will be convinced your book will be a feast.

Editors now know that you have a strong idea and that there's a book's worth of information about it. At least one sample chapter will show how well you will write the book.

After the ammunition in your introduction, your sample material is the most important part of your proposal. Your writing must deliver what your introduction promises. The last part of your proposal is the only chance you have to strut your stuff, to prove you have what it takes to write the book. A humor book must make editors laugh, a dramatic or inspirational book must move them.

Like the rest of your manuscript, the sample chapters must achieve the goals you set for them both in content and in their impact on readers. If they do, they may increase the value of your proposal by allaying an editor's anxiety about your ability to write the book.

A Q&A SESSION ON WHAT TO SUBMIT

A cartoon in *The New Yorker* shows a sedan speeding away from the scene of the crime with a police car in hot pursuit, and the driver is leaning out the window reassuring a bystander:

"I'm only doing this to support my writing."

If you want to support your writing, you will probably need to include a sample of your writing, at least until you have a track record.

The first decision you have to make about your sample text is the number of chapters you will prepare. This will depend on:

- your knowledge of the subject
- whether you have had anything published on the subject
- your track record as a writer
- the time, energy, information and other resources at your disposal
- how many sample chapters an editor has to see to become as excited as possible about your book.

Since you're working "on spec" on a proposal that may not sell, you want to minimize your time, effort and expense. The answers to the following fourteen questions will help you understand how to prepare your writing sample:

1. Can you get away with not sending a chapter?
If you've already written a book on the subject, your track record is strong enough, or if your credentials are impeccable, you may not need any sample chapters; an outline submitted with previous work may suffice.

Another circumstance in which you may not need sample material is if you have had several books published which attest to your ability to write the book you are proposing.

Teaching, running a professional practice, or staff or freelance journalism of high quality over a period of years may also be sufficient to prove your credentials. But if you don't prepare sample material, write a longer outline.

2. How many chapters should your book have?
As you string together the pieces of information that will become your book, they will fall into natural groupings that will become your chapters. Ten to twelve chapters is common for a 200- to 250-page manuscript. The longer your book, the more chapters

it will have. Once again, look at successful books on the subject as setting a standard for you to follow.

3. How long should your chapters be?

Serious books tend to have longer chapters than books aimed at a mass audience. Like the book itself, your chapters should be no longer than it takes to say what must be said. Your chapters are the building blocks of your book. Maintain a balance between making them too thin and so long that they put readers off. Similar books and your network of readers will keep you on the right track.

4. How many chapters should you send an editor?

If you were writing your first novel, agents and editors would expect to see the whole manuscript for two reasons: to prove that you can write a novel by demonstrating that you can develop plot, character and setting with maximum impact.

If you're writing a nonfiction book that you want to have the impact of a novel—a dramatic story with mounting suspense about the solution of a crime, or an inspirational book about someone who has overcome formidable obstacles to achieve a goal—an outline can't convey the emotional impact of a finished manuscript.

You can sell most books with two sample chapters, especially if you have been published. But the emotional impact of the manuscript will be stronger—and your book will probably be worth more—if an editor reads the whole manuscript.

In his book, *A Writer's Guide to Book Publishing*, AAR member Richard Balkin recommends that writers submit 20 to 25 percent of the book. Forty to fifty pages of manuscript or two sample chapters, is enough of an audition. But they must read like they are worth the advance you want for your book.

Remember: The goals of your proposal are not to waste an editor's time and to generate the maximum amount of excitement with the minimum number of words. So the criteria for deciding how much more than two chapters to send is: How much of the book are you willing to write before selling it? Will an additional chapter create enough additional excitement to justify including it?

5. When aren't two chapters necessary?
An editor doesn't have to see every exercise or recipe to know if a how-to book is publishable. If your book will be a series of chapters identical in structure and with the same kind of information, such as a travel guide, one sample chapter will suffice. For instance, if you were going to write the guidebook to Europe's ten greatest cities mentioned earlier, an editor will only have to see how you cover one city.

If you have a choice of which chapter to prepare, choose the most exciting one you can write. When you're sending only one chapter, it must be representative. It should come from the heart of the book and be a shining example of what is innovative and stimulating about your subject.

6. What if you have divided your book into three parts?
If the three parts of your book are distinctive enough, consider submitting one chapter from each part.

7. What if your book is depressing?
If your subject is depressing, try to make at least part of your sample material upbeat so that, if possible, an editor will finish reading your proposal feeling positive about the subject, your proposal and the prospect of working with you on your book.

8. What if it's a fill-in-the-blank book?
Send the whole manuscript. Librarians don't like fill-in books because their borrowers fill them in. So if your book will require written responses, ask them to use a piece of paper or a notebook unless it's essential for them to write in the book.

9. Should you send the introduction?
You may not be able to write certain chapters because they require time, travel or other resources you need an advance to obtain.

You may want to write the introductory chapter, but in a how-to book, for instance, an introduction will not demonstrate how you will treat the instructional material, which is the heart of your book. For this reason, writers often do both an introductory chapter and one representative chapter.

For most books, whether or not they will have an introductory chapter, two strong sample chapters will give both you and an editor confidence that you can and want to write about the subject. As your in-house agent whose job it is to stir up interest in your book, an editor needs that confidence to fight for your book.

If knowing the concepts in your introductory chapter is essential to understanding your outline, insert the introductory chapter at the beginning of the outline and the other sample chapter after the outline.

Just as the beginning of your proposal must hook agents and editors, the first chapter of your book must hook book buyers. It doesn't have to be long, but it must convince them that because of what you are writing and how you write it, your book will be worth their time.

10. Do the chapters have to be in sequence?
Sample chapters don't have to be from the beginning of the book or in sequence. But do make your sample material complete segments or chapters, not a part of one or more chapters. An editor will want to see how complete slices of the book read.

If, however, you are putting together a collection of some kind, and you can get pieces of every chapter but not a complete chapter, outline each chapter thoroughly, and after each outline, include at least 10 percent of the material from each chapter.

Even if you are providing complete chapters, if you have all of the recipes or exercises for your book, for example, including the best 10 percent of each chapter after each outline will help an editor envision your book.

11. Which chapters do you send?
The following cartoon appears in Jim Charlton's *Books, Books, Books*, a collection of cartoons about writing and publishing that appeared in *The New Yorker*. A man is standing at the counter of a bookstore about to buy a book and the clerk is saying to him: "You'll like this one, sir. It has a surprise ending in which the murderer turns out to be the detective."

If you have a chapter that's guaranteed to surprise editors, that's the one to send.

If you're not sure which chapters to use as samples, preparing the outline will help you decide. Certain chapters usually stand out as being easier to do and more impressive for editors to read. Getting feedback on your proposal will convince you that you've chosen well.

What if you have finished more of the book than you submit?

You will be mentioning on the resource page of the introduction how much of the manuscript is finished. If editors want to see more than you submit, they will ask you.

12. What if you haven't had anything published?

In *This Business of Writing*, Gregg Levoys wrote: "For writers who have no track record, your proposal *is* your portfolio. And it's got to sing!"

If you have had no articles or books for the general public published, and your proposal is all an editor will have to go on, you may want to submit more of the manuscript—a third to a half—depending on how ambitious the project is and how well you write.

13. What if you have finished the manuscript?

Editors are perpetually swamped. They just need enough of a sample to judge whether you can write the book. They and the other people in the house who have to review your proposal will read a small pile of pages faster than a large pile. So even if you have more, don't send it unless an editor requests it.

14. What if your book has no chapters?

If your book doesn't break up into chapters, an editor will still expect to see at least 10 percent of the completed manuscript. If you're proposing a picture book, make the project more substantial by writing an introduction to your book and providing captions and perhaps a running text.

Unless a large national audience already exists for your work, or your idea is extremely commercial, your book will need more than just illustrations. Unless they're getting your book to give as a gift, or unless they feel they must own it, browsers may not buy your book if they can finish it in the store.

Editors are print people, people of the word. They want text to explain illustrations. They also want a compelling reason to go to the effort and expense of producing a picture book. As for the illustrations you include in the proposal, they should be gorgeous and, in their diversity, representative of the range of illustrations that will be in your book.

If you have a vision of how you want your book to look and you are able to design sample pages on your computer or you can obtain the services of an experienced book designer, include a cover design (which is discussed in the next chapter) and two, two-page layouts as examples of the design you want for the book.

These are only worth including if they are of professional quality. Even if you envision a book larger than 8″ × 11″, make your sample pages 8½″ × 11″ like the rest of your proposal. They will be easier to prepare, reproduce and submit.

Understand that your publisher's sales and marketing staff expect to have the final say on how your book is presented to the public, and keep in mind that they are extremely territorial. So if you present a cover design or suggest a format for your book, it must be with the understanding that if the "S&M crowd" says it "won't fly," you will have to compromise or seek another publisher.

Now you know what editors expect to see in proposals. Once you start doing it, the pieces will start falling into place. Once you are committed to writing your proposal, your sense of excitement about it will grow as the project develops momentum and creates a life of its own. The advice in the next chapter will help you make your proposal shine.

PART THREE

Getting Your Proposal to Market

Chapter Ten

PUTTING THE PIECES TOGETHER: MAKING YOUR PROPOSAL STAND OUT

Shrinkwrapped, the book Twenty Ways to Mate: Translated From the French With Original Illustrations, *was selling like hotcakes. As he rang up yet another sale, one clerk shook his head and said to another: "You know, I've just never seen a chess book sell so well."*
—Jeff Rovin, *1,001 Great Jokes*

To help ensure that your proposal is impeccable when you submit it, this chapter will provide four ways for you to increase the salability of your proposal by submitting illustrations, clips of your work, cover art and a professional-looking document.

ILLUSTRATIONS
Illustrations add to a book's salability, but they can also make a book more expensive for your publisher, readers and you. If you will use illustrations, include the illustrations for your sample chapters.

In 1979, we sold *Raven: The Untold Story of the Rev. Jim Jones and His People* for Tim Reiterman, a reporter for the *San Francisco Examiner*, who was wounded in Guyana. Tim didn't have to account for photographs because his publisher knew that Tim could obtain whatever pictures were needed.

If your book is about a subject in the news, photographs will be available, so you don't have to include them. Just indicate where photos will appear and add the cost to your cover letter about the resources you need to complete your book.

Submit your illustrations if they will be a major element in your book. When you plan to use an illustration of a person, place, event or instructional point, indicate this in the text by typing "(Illus. x)" after mentioning what you will illustrate.

Number your illustrations consecutively. Make your pictures no larger than 8½"×11" so they will fit in with your text. Affix illustrations to 8½"×11" sheets.

Place each illustration on a separate page following the page on which you mention it. Give the illustration page the same number as the page of text preceding it followed by a letter of the alphabet: 27a, for example. If you have more than one illustration on a page, work your way through the alphabet. Underneath your illustration, indicate what number it is and provide a caption.

Four considerations will dictate how you handle captions:

1. your vision of the book
2. how successful similar books use illustrations
3. how much explanation your illustrations need
4. whether your illustrations will be grouped together or spread throughout your book.

If you're sending duplicate slides, number them and insert them in plastic sheets that hold twenty slides. Place the slide behind your proposal or in the left pocket of the folder in which you are submitting your proposal. Behind them include a page with numbered captions.

If you can scan slides, photographs and artwork into your computer and integrate them into your text, do so.

If your book will contain black-and-white photos, use 8"×10" glossies for the sample chapters. Color illustrations result in heavy production costs for publishers, so unless there's a real need for color, stick to black and white, or consider a combination of the two.

Line drawings are less expensive to produce than photographs, so consider using drawings instead. As mentioned above, let your preferences and comparable books guide you in balancing cost, effectiveness and aesthetics.

Color illustrations may be expensive to duplicate or photocopy for a multiple submission. If the illustrations are essential to the effectiveness of your proposal, submit it to just one or a few people at a time as your budget allows. Always send photocopies of artwork and duplicates of slides until your editor requests originals.

Illustrations are usually printed in one of three ways: in eight- or sixteen-page inserts on coated stock for better reproduction, scattered throughout the book on the same stock as the text to save money or a combination of the two.

Gift books are printed entirely on coated stock to enhance the quality of the illustrations and impart a more luxurious feel to the book. If it's not clear from the proposal how the illustrations should be grouped and you have strong feelings about it, describe how you see them being presented in the overview.

SAMPLE CLIPS

Outstanding samples of your published work demonstrate acceptance of your work by publications willing to publish it and the implicit acceptance of their readers. Sample clips are medals that you can brag about. Besides proving that you are a professional, they show editors what you can do.

If you have clips that will impress an editor because of their quality, length, relevance, range of subjects or the periodicals in which they appeared, include up to six of them. If it's a magazine piece, clip your article to the cover of the magazine. Originals are more effective than photocopies, but if you want to avoid the possibility of losing the originals, send photocopies.

Only send a clip or published book if it will help sell your proposal. Otherwise, wait until an editor asks to see more.

> **HOT TIP** Editors aren't impressed by small or poorly produced periodicals, which may be where a writer's early work appears. Like everything else in the proposal, the clips you submit must impress jaded New York editors. Use your judgment, but when in doubt, leave it out.

COVER ART

Effective cover art can help sell your proposal by giving editors a feel for the book and its marketability. A paperback cover or a hardcover jacket must combine art and commerce. It must be attractive, but it must also sell your book.

Whether through lack of knowledge or interest, authors don't usually get involved with designing cover art. However, if you are an artist or a photographer, or have access to one, or you are in advertising and you have a selling title and cover idea—perhaps an illustration from your book—try your hand at it.

Professionals in the field spend their lives creating cover art, and they still don't always get it right. The concept and the execution of the art and type must be of professional quality, or your artwork may backfire and give publishers a reason to reject your proposal.

Try out the preliminary sketch and the finished artwork on booksellers and other members of your professional networks before submitting it. If they say that, on a scale of one to ten, it's a ten, submit it. As with sample clips, when in doubt. . . .

Make the artwork the size of the book you envision but no larger than 8½″ × 11″ so it fits as the first page of the proposal. If you are planning a multiple submission, use artwork that will reproduce well.

HOW TO FORMAT YOUR PROPOSAL

Here is how to prepare the title page and table of contents, both of which should be typed double-spaced in upper and lower case letters.

The Title Page

The first page of your proposal will be the title page. About a third of the way down the page, in the center or along the left margin, type:

> A Proposal for
> Title (either underlined or in italics)
> Subtitle (either underlined or in italics)
> by (Guess who?)

Include your degree or your position and affiliation if relevant and impressive, for example:

> Professor of Psychology, Stanford University

If possible, add either or both of the following two lines:

> Introduction by X
> First in a Series of X Books

Near the bottom of the page, flush left, type:

Your street address
City, State, ZIP code
Area code and day and evening phone numbers
Fax number
E-mail address

The Table of Contents

The page after your title page is the table of contents for your proposal. Besides showing an editor what's ahead, this page makes the proposal look carefully organized, like a miniature version of the book it aspires to be. It will also help editors refer back to specific parts of your proposal.

List the three parts of the proposal flush left, then indent the sections of each part. At the right margin indicate the page on which each begins:

Table of Contents

If you find stories in major periodicals, such as a cover story in *Newsweek*, that make your proposal more salable, underline the relevant parts and include the articles.

If you have more than one story about yourself or rave reviews about a previous book, underline the key points and put the material in the folder separately.

You don't have to mention front matter such as a dedication, epigraph or acknowledgments in your proposal.

Although promoting your book may be the greatest challenge,

HOT TIP Editors will not expect you to design your book. They just want to be able to turn the pages as quickly as possible. We once received a proposal from someone who had gone hog-wild with type fonts and had six different typefaces on one page. This made the page look like an amateur-night attempt to dress up the proposal. Unless you possess proven design skills or have access to them, keep your proposal simple in appearance like the samples in this book.

writing it, especially if it's your first book, will take you to another level of achievement. Your devotion to your craft will help determine the reception your book receives from all of the gatekeepers who come between you and your readers. So now that you've read about content, let's zero in on style.

Chapter Eleven

GETTING THE WORDS WRITE: A STYLE GUIDE FOR YOUR PROPOSAL

Editors don't edit. We expect you agents to do that. We only acquire.
—Editor to AAR member Sandra Watt

The following three sentences are children's answers to questions they were asked in their church schools. What do they all have in common?

- The fifth commandment is humor thy father and mother.
- Christians can have only one wife. This is called mónotany.
- It is sometimes difficult to hear what is being said in church because the agnostics are so terrible.

They all show how even two or three letters in a word can transform the meaning of a sentence. Every word you write to an agent or editor counts. Narrative nonfiction that tells a story hopes to seduce readers with its style and emotional impact. However, people buy most nonfiction for information, not style.

Nonetheless, every editor who cares about good books—and that's why editors become editors—is a sucker for fine writing. You want agents and editors to read your proposal without stopping and with a growing rush of enthusiasm.

Your book will only have two basic elements: your idea and the execution of that idea. Set a literary goal for yourself: Make the execution of your idea as strong as your idea.

Craft leaps off the page instantly. Since editors and agents reject more than 95 percent of what they see, they will be delighted if after reading your first paragraph, they can say to themselves: "My God! This one can really write!"

And although style is more important in a literary biography than in a how-to book, the more pleasurable any book is to read, the better its reviews and the more word-of-mouth recommendations it generates.

When Linda Ashcroft, the author of *Wild Child*, recommends this book to other writers, she tells them, "Use his format but use your style." Good advice. Your writing will be an expression of who you are.

Make how you write as important as what you write. Make style as important as content. If you are serious about being a writer, aim to make your writing as lucid, flowing, creative, brilliant, moving, engaging, entertaining, passionate—in a word, irresistible, as you want your reviews to be.

"Wondering irresolutely what to do next, the clock struck twelve." This gem is from the indispensable guide to the prose of pros: *The Elements of Style* by William Strunk, Jr. and E.B. White. It inspires as it teaches, by example. The relative calm before starting your proposal is a propitious moment to summon your muse by (re)reading it. Put its thirty-two golden nuggets on composition and style on the wall where you write. If something's amiss with your writing, and it's not on that list, it may be covered in the pages that follow.

This advice is based on mistakes that we encounter repeatedly. Not all of it will apply to you as a writer or to your book. Listen to your muse.

ADDING VARIETY TO YOUR PROSE

Every word of your writing must inspire readers to read the next word. For this reason, avoid:

• **Long words:** Keep them simple, but if a long word is the best one to use, use it.

• **Long sentences:** Long or complex sentences slow the eye. But don't go to the other extreme. By using sentence fragments. Or a succession of short sentences.

• **Long paragraphs:** The mind revolts when confronted with unbroken, page-long blocks of copy. If you're writing for a wide audience, aim for three or four paragraphs a page, and avoid paragraphs longer than about a third of a page. Once again, use similar books as benchmarks.

However, variety is as essential a virtue in prose as brevity.

An endless succession of short words, sentences and paragraphs will read like ad copy or a formula approach to writing. The art of writing is the ability to express and structure your ideas so that every word counts. Stick with the standards set by books you admire.

Between your overview, outline and sample chapters, an editor may read the same information three times. Avoid repeating yourself if you can. If you can't, vary your wording.

Assume the editor knows only what the average American knows about the subject; terms, concepts and explanations must be clear. Avoid cuteness and gratuitous humor.

Excite your readers' senses—sight, sound, touch, taste and smell—to breathe life into the people, places and events you depict. Let the accumulation of significant details make what you write about convincing and a joy to read.

Like an anecdote, dialogue is action. It breaks up the narrative and enlivens your prose as it develops the story, characters and atmosphere. People enjoy reading about other people. So if it suits the kind of book you are writing, humanize your book by writing about people.

OVERCOMING REPETITION WITH RESTRAINT

Using a word, sentence structure or punctuation, then using it again, and then, since it comes to mind quickly, using it again, is a nasty habit that unwary writers are prey to. The repetition makes it stand out like a writing tic, a literary hiccough.

Given the richness of the language, this suggests either a lack of writing skill or an unwillingness to find the most felicitous way to express a thought.

If you lapse into the repetition of a word, sentence structure or punctuation, avoid the offending usage altogether so you won't be tempted to succumb or limit yourself to using the culprit only once every twenty pages. It's an easier cure for hiccoughs than drinking a glass of water with your head upside down.

If you use two or more nouns or verbs together, make sure that all of them fit the rest of the sentence. I managed to provide an example of this mistake in a first draft of this manuscript: "For a more professional look, greater protection and the possibility of resubmitting the proposal elsewhere, insert it. . . ."

The preposition *for* has three nouns as objects: *look, protection* and *possibility*. Unfortunately, you can't say *the possibility of*. You will see how I revised the sentence in the section on how to submit your proposal.

⚡ **HOT TIP** One way to know if your words and sentences are as smooth as you want them to be: Read them aloud to hear how they sound. But don't write like you talk unless you want to create the effect of speech. When speaking, we take liberties with words and grammar that are acceptable, but come across as improvised, rather than carefully written, when they appear on paper.

WORDS TO AVOID

Disambiguate.

—A word the Pentagon coined meaning to clarify

Avoid the adverb *obviously*. Don't tell an editor what is obvious.

Avoid adverbs and adjectives. Write with nouns and verbs.

Avoid the verb *to be*, if you can find a stronger verb. Avoid sentences that begin *It is* or *There is/are*.

Avoid *this chapter* or *this book*; use *the*.

Avoid weak, indefinite words like *much, maybe, probably, perhaps, few, some, something, anything, thing(s), many, a lot, lots of, plenty of, numerous, almost, quite, little, awhile* and *several*. Be accurate, definite and specific without using the word *specific*.

Avoid obscure, out-of-the-ordinary words like *drollery* unless they are part of your style and you use them throughout your proposal.

Avoid the word *recently*; it won't be for long.

Avoid weak verbs. Use *can* for *could*; *will* for *would, might,* or *should*; *is* for *seems to be*. Readers want to be informed by an authority, so write like one! The more forceful your statements the better, particularly in the overview, when you're trying to sell your idea and yourself to an editor. Don't pussyfoot around. Be accurate, but be bold.

Avoid too many *ands*. Because computers make it so easy to add words, writers sometimes just string words together that are redundant or do not fit the sentence.

Avoid negative words or expressions. As *The Elements of Style* says: "Put statements in positive form."

Avoid sexist words or phrasing. Use *excel in* for *master, humanity* for *man* or *mankind*. Avoid the he/she problem by using the plural *they*.

Avoid trendy buzz words like *mode, process* or *in process, via, viable, reader-* or *user-friendly, baby boomer* or *impact* as a verb.

Avoid *utilize* for *use*.

Avoid *due to*; use *because of*.

Avoid *ongoing* for *continuing*.

Avoid writing *different ways* or *various ways*. Enumerate the ways or tell how many ways there are to x. If you're discussing more than one way, they must be different or various.

Avoid writing *three years ago* or *three years from now*; it may date your proposal. Give the year.

Avoid jargon. You may be a psychologist or a computer hacker but not all of your readers are. Don't make your vocabulary a barrier to communication. It's not, if you'll forgive the word, appropriate.

Avoid *interrelated* and *interconnected*; they are redundant.

Avoid exaggerating anything. Don't let your accuracy become suspect.

Avoid superlatives unless they are warranted.

Avoid all-encompassing words like *all, every* or *never*, unless they are accurate.

Avoid creating new words or bulky word combinations united by hyphens or slash marks. Don't take liberties with the language; it's a glorious instrument which already has enough keys to create all of the color, texture, vitality, variety and emotion you need.

Avoid citing a dictionary and defining terms; it comes across as academic.

Avoid inevitable words. If you're writing a book about sex, avoid the word. It's going to show up often enough anyway when there's no alternative. Use a synonym, write around it or just leave it out. Readers know what you're talking about.

Avoid imprecise words. Editors are word people. How well you choose your words will be important to them.

Avoid cliches like the plague. Don't use expressions you are used to hearing or seeing in print; be original.

Avoid ordinary, overworked, lifeless words, phrases and images. Strive to make your writing vivid and colorful. This doesn't mean that you should never use warhorses like *show, tell, make, give, get, do, put* (to mean *say*), *good, very, interesting* or *fascinating*, but your goal is to infuse your prose with as much feeling, resonance and vitality as your subject allows.

Avoid saying *the reader*. You will have more than one so use the plural.

Avoid *etc.* You will slow editors down by forcing them to think about what it refers to. Either include the whole list or use part of the list and preface it with *like* or *such as*.

Avoid the word *City* in *New York City*.

Avoid the abbreviation *U.S.* Editors will assume you're talking about this country. If you need it, spell it out.

Avoid abbreviations such as *i.e.* and *e.g.* that are suitable for business memos unless, like P.M., they are accepted in formal prose. For the same reason, avoid using *per* for *a*.

Type the subtitles of chapters in upper and lower case.

Avoid putting words in capital letters for emphasis; it looks amateurish. Let your choice of words and how you position them create the desired effect.

> **HOT TIP** When you send your proposal and later your manuscript to be critiqued, include a note telling readers what you need feedback on. The more specific and thorough your request is, the better the feedback you will receive. Ask them to rate parts of your proposal that you want responses on, such as jokes and anecdotes and your proposal as a whole, on a scale of one to ten. Include as nice a red pen as your budget allows.

NUMBERS

If you're writing a how-to book in which numbers are important, such as this one, use words for the numbers one to ninety-nine and for numbers at the beginning of sentences. Otherwise, digits are acceptable. For other kinds of books, follow the usage in comparable books. (The observant will notice that the publisher of this book uses a somewhat different approach to numbers.)

Don't mention cents or the lack of them—.00—when discussing money. Stick to round dollar figures.

Your readers will get bogged down in specific numbers unless they really need to know them. Use your judgment in deciding whether to write *twenty-two* rather than *more than twenty*, or *twenty-four* instead of *almost twenty-five* or just *twenty-five* if absolute accuracy isn't necessary. The larger the number, the easier it is to remember round numbers.

PUNCTUATION AND ITALICS
Avoid underlining for emphasis. Underline the names of books and periodicals unless your computer's printer can print them in italics.

Avoid exclamation points; unless really needed, they look like you're trying to force an emotion out of the reader.

Avoid parentheses in the overview and outline. If something's worth saying, say it; if not, leave it out.

One dash mark is a hyphen for linking words or dividing them into syllables. If you wish to use a dash to set off a word or phrase, type two hyphens—with no spaces between the dashes and what surrounds them.

Hyphenate two-or-more words used to modify a noun, when the hyphenation clarifies the meaning. Examples are *black-and-white photos*, *fifteen-page document* and *high-quality work*. However, avoid hyphenating an adjective and an adverb ending in *ly*: *beautifully written*.

Use quote marks if you're quoting someone and always make it clear whom you're quoting and why. Otherwise, avoid them.

Use a single quote mark as an apostrophe or for a quote within a quote. For example: Then he smiled and recalled, "She said to me: 'You don't say!' "

Use a comma after the next-to-last part of a list only if omitting it will cause confusion.

The ultimate commandment for nonfiction:
Make your prose as enjoyable to read as it is informative.

LESS IS MORE, MORE IS A BORE
Think of writing as having two stages: writing for fact and writing for impact. First you have to write something, anything

down, and then massage it into final form.

After you have the information down, add The Pleasure Factor. As you revise making every word right, enhance your prose with grace notes—humor, beauty, passion, inspiration, felicitous turns of phrase—anything that will add feeling and aesthetic value to your information.

Grace notes are the value that you add to your information. They are an essential element in building the humorous, dramatic, spiritual, inspirational, intellectual, even life-changing impact that you want your book to have.

Someone once said: "The sculptor produces the beautiful statue by chipping away such parts of the marble block as are not needed—it is a process of elimination."

Fine writing stands out because of its lack of faults. Books endure in part because their authors had the taste to know when a word, sentence or idea didn't feel right, and the perseverance to revise their work until it sparkled.

First-time authors may find it difficult to believe, but when it comes to prose, less is more. Good writing is simple, not unnecessarily flashy; direct, not flowery; and concise. Your proposal should tell editors everything you want them to know but in as few words as possible.

For example, avoid throat-clearing prefaces to a statement such as "It is interesting that . . ." or "I truly believe that. . . ." Tell your readers what you want them to know, then move on.

At its best, writing also has passion, vision and vigor. Bantam executive editor Toni Burbank once remarked about a manuscript: "There was nothing wrong with it, but there was nothing right with it either."

Author Cyra McFadden once lamented about another failed effort: "The prose just lay there, dead on the page." Make your writing sing to an editor, who should be your toughest yet most sympathetic critic, and if you have a salable idea and a strong promotion plan, your proposal will sell.

TWO MORE STEPS TO AN IRRESISTIBLE PROPOSAL

Once you have written your proposal as well as you can, it's time to find out if you're right. Let's look at the final steps for ensuring that your proposal is irresistible.

Let other people read your proposal

By the time you've finished your proposal, you will need a respite. You may find yourself developing tunnel vision which impairs your ability to judge your work objectively. You may be so close to it that you can't distinguish its faults from its virtues. If you revise a passage often enough, you know it so well that you start to see what's not there. Now's the time to give yourself a break and share your proposal with readers who can advise you on how to improve it:

• Friends and family. You need and deserve encouragement. If you want a pat on the back, let your friends and family give it to you. Unless they have hidden resentments and use criticizing your proposal as the means to express them, they will tell you they like it because they like you. After all, what are friends and family for?

If you want sound advice, try these readers:

• Potential buyers of the book. They may not know good writing, but they know what they like. Would they buy your book if they found it in a bookstore? See if you can enlist booksellers to render an opinion.

• Literate, objective readers who can tell you what's wrong with your proposal as well as what's right with it.

• Experts in the field you are writing about.

• Readers who disagree with you if you're presenting a controversial idea. Find members of the opposition to go over your proposal and try to poke holes in it. You may not convert them but you might earn their respect and avoid embarrassing yourself later.

• And most valuable of all, the most critical critic, a devil's advocate. A devil's advocate is a mentor whose taste and judgment you respect and in whose knowledge of books and writing you have absolute confidence.

A devil's advocate can combine truth with charity and while analyzing the overall vision and development of the book, can spot every word, punctuation mark, sentence structure, idea, character and incident that can be improved or removed. Devil's advocates are worth their weight in royalties.

See if you can get one or more of these angels to read this book before reading your proposal so they can judge if it covers all the bases.

Chapter thirteen discusses the importance of building networks of people in the field you're writing about and others in and out of the publishing world who are interested in your work.

Experts on the subject can give you advice that agents and editors can't because they're not experts on most subjects. For everyone who reads it, however, your proposal will be a Rorschach test. They will each spot only what they can see when they read it. Collectively, their responses and your responses to them will make your proposal, and later your manuscript, signifcantly better.

> ⚡ **HOT TIP** Telling writers you know that you will be happy to review their proposals will give you experience critiquing prose and help you build a network of writers willing to return the favor.

Since people like to see their names in print, promise readers autographed copies of the book and that you will mention them on the acknowledgments page.

Critique groups. Join or start a critique group, a tableful of writers that meets online or in person and discusses its members' work. Working with more experienced writers will prove more productive.

Calling a book doctor. If you don't have anybody nearby or online, hire a freelance editor, a "book doctor" who can show you a list of published nonfiction books aimed at the general public for which the editor worked on the proposal. Ask if editors will let you talk to their clients or the agents who represent them. At this writing, freelance editors charge either a flat fee for an hourly rate that ranges from $25 to more than $100 an hour.

When you find an editor you want to work with, ask him or her if they have read this book so they understand what you are trying to write. Then get an assessment of the proposal and an estimate of what it will cost to edit it and a revision based on the editor's recommendations.

Check the listings in *Literary Market Place* in your library if your publishing network doesn't lead you to any editors. Another source for first-rate editors is the Independent Editors Group (IEG). For a membership roster, contact:

Independent Editors Group
% Jerry Gross
63 Grand Street
Croton-on-Hudson, New York 10530-2518

If you decide that you would like a ghostwriter to write or collaborate on the book, an agent or editor may be able to recommend one.

Integrate changes into a final revision

Since reactions are subjective, receiving more than one will prepare you for the range of responses your book will arouse. Be prepared to sift conflicting and even confusing suggestions and follow only the advice that makes sense to you.

Trust your instincts. Once you have sorted out the opinions of others and feel ready to return to your proposal with a fresh eye, go over it again and revise it one more time. When you're sure your proposal is ready, it's time to send your baby out into the real world.

FORMATTING YOUR PROPOSAL

Remember the adage: "You never get a second chance to make a first impression"? The appearance of your proposal reflects the professionalism with which you are approaching the agent or editor, the subject and your career. It's the tangible evidence of the care you will lavish on your manuscript. Consequently, the impression it makes of you affects readers' reactions to your proposal.

Make your proposal a document that looks like it's worth the advance you want for it. Agents and editors know from experience that there's a relationship between how writers submit manuscripts and how they write them.

Here is a list of fourteen dos and don'ts on preparing your proposal:

1. Type your proposal on one side of $8\frac{1}{2}'' \times 11''$ 20-pound bond paper.
2. Type twenty-five sixty-character lines, about 250 words on a page.
3. Type everything, including quotes and anecdotes, double-spaced, not one and a half spaces.

4. Don't add extra spaces between paragraphs.
5. Avoid "widows," a subhead at the bottom of a page or the last line of a chapter at the top.
6. Use a standard, serif, pica (ten characters to an inch) type.
7. If you're writing with a typewriter, use a new ribbon and clean keys, and set $1\frac{1}{4}''$ margins on the top and sides of the page.
8. Don't justify the right margin; the designer will do that.
9. Type your name, address, day and evening phone numbers, fax number and e-mail address on your title page.
10. Use running heads. Type your last name and the first key word from the title separated by a slash mark so they appear at the upper left margin of each page. Type the number of the page on the same line, flush right:

Larsen/Write   7

11. Number pages consecutively from one to the end of the proposal, not by section or chapter, so that if your proposal is dropped, it will be easy to put the pages back in order.
12. Proofread your proposal carefully and get an eagle-eyed friend to check your work. If you're using a computer, proofread a printout to catch what you may have missed on the screen, especially those extra spaces between words that can sneak in when you revise.

HOT TIP Here are two tips for proofreading. Run your index finger under each word as you read it aloud softly to yourself. Proofread your proposal from back to front so you can concentrate on the words and not be seduced into reading it.

Elise NeeDell Babcock, whose proposal is in the back of the book, has another way to read a proposal out of order. She mixes up the pages and reads them in five-page chunks.

---

13. Always submit material without staples or any form of binding. Paper clips are acceptable, but they leave indentations on the paper.
14. For a more professional look and greater protection in case

you have to resubmit the proposal, insert it in the right side of a colored, double-pocket construction-paper portfolio. You can use the left pocket for writing samples, illustrations and supporting documents. Put a self-adhesive label on the front of the folder with your title and name.

15. Make everything in the proposal, including artwork, no larger than $8\frac{1}{2}'' \times 11''$. This makes it easy to reproduce and submit.

In every day's pile of submissions, every agent receives letters and proposals that don't follow these guidelines. So one simple way to make your proposal stand out is to make it look impeccable.

Now, on to conquer the marketplace!

Chapter Twelve

THREE WAYS TO TEST-MARKET YOUR IDEA

I'm easy to please. I only want the best.
　　—Stanley (Neiman-) Marcus, unintentionally speaking for all agents and editors.

B efore trying out your idea on an agent or editor, try it out on the people you want to buy your book. Here are three ways to test-market your idea.

GIVE TALKS OR SEMINARS ABOUT IT

If your book will lend itself to being promoted with talks, readings or seminars, start doing them as soon as you have gathered enough information about your subject to make a well-informed, enjoyable presentation. If your book will have illustrations, use them in the talk.

The parts of your presentation can become the chapters of your book. Books generate talks. At the same time, the information gathered for talks generates books. My books on proposals and agents grew partly out of the talks we give.

Making presentations about your subject will enable you to:

* build your passion for the subject
* generate humor, anecdotes and ideas for revisions of your books by thinking and talking about them, and listening to your audiences
* receive instant feedback on how audiences respond to the subject and to you so that you can find the most felicitous way to structure and express your ideas
* build advance publicity and a market for the book
* see if you enjoy talking about the subject enough to make it a way of life

- experience a trial run of what you will be doing to promote your book
- predict—by the number of people who come to hear you and their response—the reception that awaits your book
- increase your credibility
- build your professional networks
- impress agents and editors
- develop your confidence in your ability to write your proposal and your book
- use an advance order form to sell the book as you approach the publication date.

You may even find an agent or publisher for your book, especially if you invite likely prospects. Even if they don't come, you'll hear from them if the idea interests them. (Give them a clue: mention that you're writing a book in the promotional copy and at the talk.)

Most nonfiction writers face The Promotion Paradox
How well you speak is far more important than how well you write. Nobody else cares who writes your book. Nobody expects celebrity biographies to be written by celebrities, but their promotional abilities are vital to their books' success.

Your asset is the knowledge you have to share. You may write your book yourself, use an editor or "book doctor" to help you, collaborate with a writer or hire a ghostwriter. You won't earn royalties based on *how* you write your book, only on how well it sells.

If the writing captures your distinctive voice in an engaging way, so much the better. However, unless you are writing a serious book, a reference work, a novelty or gift book or another kind of book that doesn't lend itself to author promotion, your ability to promote your work is essential to its success. And speaking is usually an essential part of an author's promotional arsenel.

Speaking gives you the chance to test-market titles
Try to make the title for your talk the title for your book. The goal is for them to create synergy. They can help sell each other,

the subsidiary rights your book generates, and the spin-off books with related titles that your first book builds an audience for.

Every town has organizations that
meet regularly and need speakers
Read books on speaking and join Toastmasters to polish your skills. When you're ready, join the National Speakers Association, based in Tempe, Arizona, with chapters around the country.

Not all books lend themselves to speaking, but these two suggestions will help you expand the possibilities:

- Develop your skill at slanting your talks for different kinds of audiences. Professional speakers must constantly "customize" their presentations. You can, too.
- If your book doesn't lend itself to talks, find a subject that you would enjoy giving crowd-pleasing talks about and give them. The publicity material for the talk can include a mention of your book, and you can sell copies afterwards. And you may be on your way to developing your next book.

WRITE ARTICLES ABOUT YOUR SUBJECT

Getting an article about your subject published can be an effective method to prove the interest in your idea. Researching it will enable you to prove to yourself that there's a book in the subject.

Writing the article will give you a feeling for how well you handle the subject, how you can solve the problems involved in writing the book, how long it will take and how much you will enjoy writing it. The experience will help you decide if you are a sprinter—an article writer—or a marathoner able to go the distance.

An article can be the embryo from which your book evolves.

HOT TIP If you need to interview hard-to-reach people for the book, they will be more agreeable to talking if you're on assignment for a newspaper or magazine than if you're just doing research for an unsold book.

The periodical you sell the article to, the price you get for it and the reaction from editors and readers will help you gauge your book's appeal. Responses from readers may correct mistakes and provide new facts, sources and lines of inquiry. Having an article published about the subject of your book helps to establish your credibility as a writer and an authority with publishers.

One or more articles that are long enough and strong enough can function as sample material. Your article may even sell your book. When they read, agents and editors always hope to discover writers and ideas. If your article attracts an editor, you may not even need to write a proposal.

An article involves risk because another writer may also decide to do a book on the subject. To lessen this danger and stimulate responses from readers, agents and editors, ask the editor of the publication to state on the first page of the article with your credits that it is from a book in progress. This suggests that you have a head start and will deter potential competitors while attracting agents and editors.

Since your proposal may not sell, placing an article will help offset the cost of your time and research. If the article is popular enough, it may lead to additional articles on the subject, which will aid your research and increase the chances of selling the idea as a book.

Keep in mind, though, that magazines may offer less for an article than they would for first-serial rights that enable them to excerpt your book before it is published. The best time for articles based on your book to appear is when books are in the stores, so that readers who like the article will buy your book.

Selling articles long before publication may hinder first-serial sales when the time comes. This is particularly true with exposes containing startling revelations. You can only let the cat out of the bag once.

To learn more about writing articles, check with your networks, writing magazines and books that cover the subject, including *Writer's Market*.

PUBLISH THE BOOK YOURSELF

In his best-seller *Megatrends*, John Naisbitt wrote that America is evolving from an either/or society to a multiple-option society.

> ⚡ **HOT TIP** If your advance won't cover your expenses, selling articles based on the book or serializing the book in a magazine or in noncompeting newspapers will help make up the difference. Depending on where your work appears, this can be can be a powerful piece of ammunition in your promotion plan.
>
> Sell only first-time North American rights and no electronic rights to articles that will become part of your book. If this is your first book, you may find the prospect of writing it less daunting if you look at it as a series of articles.

This is certainly true when it comes to getting your books published. You have more options for getting your books published than ever. Thanks to the accessibility of desktop publishing and short-run printing, tens of thousands of writers are publishing their own books. This is the ultimate way to test-market your book.

Here are two approaches to doing it:

• You can single-space the manuscript and have it printed back to back and inexpensively bound. Even if a publisher has bought your book, this will be an effective way to test-market your manuscript. Call it a "Special Limited Readers' Edition," and include a page asking for feedback and maybe offering a free autographed copy of the publisher's edition in exchange for suggestions.

You can also use this edition to obtain quotes for the publisher's edition. You and your publisher will decide when you will stop selling your edition so it won't interfere with the new book.

Your manuscript may cost $25 or more to copy and bind. But your goal is not to make a profit from the photocopied edition; it's to use it to obtain feedback and quotes.

• You can make an all-out self-publishing effort and create the book you've dreamed about. Self-publishing is a major trend because of a myth and a reality.

The myth is that it's impossible to find an agent or publisher to look at your book, that the New York publishing world is a fortress impossible for new writers to penetrate. (The truth is that agents and editors arrive at work every day hoping to

> ⚡ **HOT TIP** The best way to write your proposal is to write your book. Outlining your book will be easier because you will know what each chapter will contain. You can pick the two strongest sample chapters because you will have all of the chapters to choose from. If time and money don't concern you and your faith in your book is strong enough to overcome the possibility that it may not sell, then go to it!

become excited by new books and new writers.) The reality is that self-publishing has many advantages that can be summed up in one word: control.

If you self-publish:

- You have complete control over the content, format, design, timing, production, pricing and marketing of your book.
- You own all subsidiary rights, including film, foreign and electronic rights.
- You make more profit on every copy.
- You can sell the book to a publisher when and if you wish.

If you publish your book, you'll wind up with a lot a books in your garage, but you'll work hard to sell them because you want to park your car. If you work hard enough, publishers may come to you.

One editor has said: "If you can sell two thousand copies a month for eight months, I want to see it." Other editors will not need as strong a track record. If you test-market your book and you sell enough copies by yourself, you will prove that the book works, and a publisher will buy it.

If you decide to sell your self-published book to a publisher, you will still need the first part of the proposal, the introduction, along with sales figures and information about subsidiary-rights sales. Indicate any changes needed in a new edition, how many manuscript pages there will be and how many months it will take you to finish them. Also indicate whether you will be giving film or a disk of your book to the publisher for production purposes. Include reviews and articles about the book.

Greg Godek, who drove around the country in his specially

painted van, sold more than one million copies of his book *1,001 Ways to Be Romantic*. However, Greg acknowledged that he spent 5 percent of his time writing his book and 95 percent of his time and $600,000 selling it.

Although technology has spurred a surge in self-publishing, it is a venerable tradition in American letters. When self-publishing guru Dan Poynter gives workshops, he hands out a list of well-known authors who have published their own work, including Walt Whitman, Henry David Thoreau, Edgar Allan Poe and Mark Twain.

The One-Minute Manager, What Color is Your Parachute?, The Celestine Prophecy, Mutant Message Down Under and *The Christmas Box* were all best-sellers and originally self-published books.

The Christmas Box sold for $4.2 million, which is at this writing a record sum for a self-published book, all the more remarkable because it only included North American hardcover rights!

If you generate enough publicity and sales through your efforts, publishers will be eager to buy the rights to publish your book. If your book is professionally designed and edited, the publisher may be able to just change the cover and the front matter and print it as is.

The two leading guides to self-publishing are Dan Poynter's *The Self-Publishing Manual: How to Write, Print and Sell Your Own Book* and *The Complete Guide to Self-Publishing* by Tom and Marilyn Ross. The authors also present classes on self-publishing and are valuable resources for the latest information on the subject. For more information, contact:

Dan Poynter
P.O. Box 8206
Santa Barbara, CA 93118-8206
Tel: (805) 968-7277
Fax: (805) 968-1379
E-mail: Dan Poynter@Parapublishing.com
Web site: http://www.Parapublishing.com

Tom and Marilyn Ross
P.O. Box 1306
Buena Vista, CO 81211-1306

Tel: (719) 395-4790
Fax: (710) 395-8374
E-mail: SPAN@span-assn.org

Another source of information is:

Publishers Marketing Association (PMA)
627 Aviations Way
Manhattan Beach, CA 90266
Tel: (310) 372-2732
Fax: (310) 374-3342
E-mail: PMAOnline@AOL.com
Web site: http://www.pma-online.org

PMA presents a two-day workshop at BookExpo America, the annual booksellers convention.

For a free publishing kit, contact:

Morris Publishing
3212 East Highway 30
Kearney, NE 68847
Tel: (800) 650-7888
Fax: (308) 237-0263

Literary Market Place, available at the library, provides comprehensive listings of products and services for publishers. Self-publishers have access to more resources than ever before. In the next chapter, you will learn about four additional options for getting your book published.

Chapter Thirteen

SELLING YOUR PROPOSAL FAST FOR TOP DOLLAR

Embrace failure. Success is just moving from failure to failure with enthusiasm.
—Speaker Scott Friedman

There's a *New Yorker* cartoon showing Charles Dickens sitting across a desk from an editor with a manuscript between them, and the editor is saying, "Make up your mind, Mr. Dickens. Was it either the best of times or the worst of times? It could scarcely have been both."

Depending on how you look at it, it was and it is. New writers confront a paradox: Like agents, publishers must find new writers to survive, yet, breaking into the business with a big publisher continues to become more difficult.

On the other hand, if your book takes off, the "upside potential" editors live in hope for is far greater than ever. *The Road Less Traveled, Men are from Mars, Women are from Venus* and *The Seven Habits of Highly Effective People* have all enjoyed worldwide sales of more than ten million copies.

So if self-publishing doesn't tempt you, one of the following four alternatives will:

• If you are an experienced designer or have access to one, you can package your book by providing a publisher with a disk ready for the printer or with bound books.

• You can pay part of the publishing costs to a subsidy publisher or all of the costs to a vanity publisher. This will guarantee that your book will be published, but it will have no credibility in the publishing community.

• You can find a publisher yourself.

• You can hire an agent to find a publisher for you.

There was a cartoon in *The Wall Street Journal* showing a fortune-teller sitting across a table from a literary type with a crystal ball between them. The fortune-teller is saying: "You will write the great American novel, but you will never find an agent."

SEVEN WAYS TO FIND THE AGENT OR PUBLISHER YOU NEED

If writers chose their agents and publishers as carefully as they chose their cars, they'd get more mileage out of their books. The following seven suggestions will help you find the publisher or agent who will increase your book's mileage.

Your publishing and "field" networks

Build your publishing network of writers, editors, writers' organizations, writing teachers, booksellers, librarians, reviewers, publishers' sales reps and publicists. Ask writers for recommendations to their agents or editors. Join writers' organizations. The online publishing community is flourishing.

Get to know every key person in the field you're writing about in the media, academia and government, as well as professionals in the trade. Ask your networks about agents and publishers. Make knowing all the professionals that you can in publishing and your field a lifelong quest. You know you've "arrived" when new writers start asking *you* for help.

> O'Connor's Rule of 250
> Each of us has 250 friends, family members, colleagues, associates and critics. And each of those 250 in turn has 250 of their own and so on.
> —Richard F.X. O'Connor

You have two sets of networks: direct and indirect. Your direct network is everyone you know, your indirect network is everyone they know. Your professional networks are essential to your success. Beside offering help in finding an agent or publisher, they can give you feedback on your ideas, titles, writing and promotion plans.

Your networks can give you quotes for your books and speaking engagements. They can connect you to other members of the network. You can exchange mailing lists. They may be able to sell copies of your book at their seminars and do seminars with you. Ask booksellers about agents and about which publishers turn out good books and promote them well.

⚡ **HOT TIP** Start a mastermind group, usually a handful of professionals, not necessarily in writing or publishing, who meet regularly by phone or mail and act as a board of directors for each other.

In some groups, members give themselves goals to accomplish before the next meeting, one member makes a note of them, and members are held accountable for meeting their goals. This is a very powerful idea. One of our authors quadrupled his earnings after the first meeting with his mastermind group.

The Association of Authors' Representatives (AAR)
The 350 literary and play agents in AAR are the best single source of experienced, reputable agents. Members are obligated to follow the AAR's code of ethics. The directories below indicate when an agent is a member of AAR.

Directories
The following directories vary in the kind and the amount of information they provide. Two quick tips:

1. Check what several of them include about the same agency.

2. Stability is another virtue of AAR members. If you are contacting an agent who is not a member of AAR, especially if the agent is outside of New York, call to verify the listing.

• *Writer's Guide to Book Editors, Publishers, and Literary Agents 1997-1998* by Jeff Herman, AAR (Prima). You can find out what kinds of books publishers and editors do by calling the editor in chief's assistant or by consulting the *Writer's Guide.* Because editors change jobs several times during their careers, verify Jeff's listings.

• The *1999 Guide to Literary Agents* (Writer's Digest Books).

Lists more than five hundred agents and includes many helpful articles.

• *Literary Agents: A Writer's Guide* by Adam Begley (-Penguin) is published in association with the New York-based group Poets and Writers. After a solid, systematic explanation of how agents work and how to find one, this guide contains a listing of almost two hundred agents who do not charge to read manuscripts.

• *Literary Market Place 1999 (LMP): The Directory of the American Book Publishing Industry with Industry Yellow Pages*, which is in your library, is the annual all-inclusive trade directory of publishing by R.R. Bowker, the publisher of *Publishers Weekly*. The listings include basic information on five hundred agents and the interests of publishers of all kinds that do three or more books a year.

• *Writer's Market*, an annual sold in bookstores, also lists publishers. Since it is published for writers, it goes into more detail about publishers' needs and requirements.

• *The Writer's Handbook*, which first appeared in 1936, is edited and published annually by Sylvia Burack, editor of *The Writer*. *The Handbook* lists the names and addresses of more than 150 agents, and also includes articles about all kinds of writing.

Literary events
Writing classes, seminars, conferences and book festivals present opportunities to meet or learn about agents and editors. Readings, lectures and book signings may also yield leads.

Magazines
Either subscribe to *Publishers Weekly (PW)* or read it at the library, but track the publishers who are doing books on your subject. The spring, summer and fall announcement issues will be particularly helpful. *Writer's Digest* and *The Writer* do annual publisher roundups.

PW also has a "Hot-Deals" column that describes agents' sales, a clue to how effective they are. You will also get a feeling for what publishers are buying. *The Writer, Writer's Digest, Poets & Writers* and other writing magazines sometimes have articles by and about agents.

Publishers' catalogs

Hardcover and trade paperback publishers produce catalogs which they send to booksellers and libraries, and which their sales reps use to sell their lists of books. Libraries receive them, and you can request them free from publishers. Catalogs will enable you to learn about what's being published.

If you think the editor of a book you see in a catalog might be receptive to your book, call the editorial department and ask who the editor is. Then make the connection. Some publishers' catalogs contain the names of the agents who control subsidiary rights on their clients' books.

Books

The research you have done on competing and complementary books will come in handy now. Check the acknowledgment page of your favorite books and those related to yours. Grateful authors thank their editors and agents.

These seven suggestions will generate a list of prospects for you to query.

HOUSE HUNTING FOR AN INDEPENDENT PRESS

Your book could be published by a small or large house, a regional or national publisher, a scholarly or university press or a religious publisher.

The economics of publishing make it difficult for big publishers to continue the tradition of nursing writers along through several losing efforts until they build an audience, write their break-out book and hit the best-seller list.

This change has created the opportunity for small independent presses and university presses. University presses were established as nonprofits to publish books by scholars for scholars. However, they and the independent presses are also under growing financial pressure. So they have taken on more of the opportunity of developing new writers by publishing books that are not commercial enough for the big houses. And they acquire most of their books directly from writers.

The founder of a small, now-defunct house in San Francisco spoke for all small publishers when he proclaimed his philosophy of publishing: "I see it, I love it, I publish it."

The nature of your book and the market for it will determine how many choices you have in choosing a publisher. If it's a guidebook to Seattle, look for a publisher like Sasquatch who specializes in regional books.

If it's an instruction book about karate, you need to find a mainstream publisher who does martial-arts books or a press that specializes in them. If it's a subject such as a biography of a lesser-known writer with a small market, it will more likely be right for a small or academic press.

Small houses have to sell fewer copies to break even so they are more likely to succumb to their passion for a book, regardless of how commercial it may be.

Small publishers have their advantages over their large competitors:

• They have smaller monthly overheads so they can be more open-minded and adventurous about the projects they take on, and they're open to taking a chance on new writers.

• They encourage writers to become more involved with the publishing process.

• Because they cannot afford as many failures as big houses, every book they do is more important to them.

Fewer people are involved, and you may be working with the owners of the house who are committed to what they're doing. They offer less up front, and you may make less in the long run, but your personal satisfaction may be greater. The number of small publishers grows every year, so there are always more potential homes for your book.

THE VIEW FROM MADISON AVENUE

Something exciting is going on in New York all the time, most of it unsolved.

—Johnny Carson

It's been estimated that agents supply 80 percent of the books put out by the major houses. That means they buy 20 percent of their books directly from writers. That's thousands of books a year.

An editor toiling at a Big Apple conglomerate once confessed to us: "Big authors are boring. The joy is in working with new authors." Editors at large houses are just as eager as those at small houses to discover promising new writers, but for them, the stakes are higher.

Large houses have high overheads and need books that maintain them, so their passion for a book is tempered by their concern for the bottom line. But if your book will have a large national audience and you can give it continuing national impact through your promotional efforts, major houses will be glad to hear from you. They have the resources to provide bigger advances and better promotion and distribution than small houses. Their books receive more attention from booksellers, reviewers and sub-rights buyers.

But communication within large houses may not be good, and unless yours is one of the company's lead books, you will probably be disappointed with the attention you and your book receive. You may be better served if your book is a big book at a small house rather than a small book at a big one.

Size is not the only factor in choosing a publisher. Editors have their own tastes, publishers their own character. Whatever the vision of the entrepreneurs who start publishing houses, they learn through trial and error.

Over time, they develop widely varying standards for how literary, commercial, serious, practical and well-illustrated they expect their books to be. Changing market conditions can bend these criteria as houses respond to what sells. For example, rising cover prices and the competition books face for readers' time created the trend toward shorter books.

Publishers may be reluctant to publish in a field in which they've had no experience and will probably avoid a book if they've had a bad experience with a similar book.

Since you can't really tell whether a publisher will be right for you and your book by its size, its location or its books, and you are after the best possible editor, publisher and deal for your book, you may want to find a literary agent.

Nonetheless, whether you approach agents or publishers, big or small, expect rejections, at least at first. Console yourself with the words of one senior editor: "Editors don't judge books, they choose them," and there will be times when "the plug doesn't fit the socket." This is also true for agents, so you have to keep plugging until you find the right socket.

Whether you try to sell it yourself or enlist the help of an agent, the goal is to get your proposal into the hands of the right editor at the right house at the right time.

If you sell your book yourself, find out by phone, by mail or through a directory who the right editor is for your book. Then send it to as many editors as you can find. Depending upon the market for your book, that can be five or fifty.

If no publisher takes it, try writing articles about the subject or go on to your next project. And as Jane Adams, the author of *How to Sell What You Write* advises, don't regard unsold work as a loss, look at it as inventory that one day will sell.

The relationships between you and your agent, editor and publisher are working marriages. To help you decide on the prospects for matrimonial bliss, visit them if you can.

If your book is good enough, anybody can sell it because any likely publisher will buy it. Many first-time authors are so excited to have their first book published that who publishes it or the terms of the deal are insignificant details. So you have to decide whether any "yes" or only the best possible "yes" will do.

HOW AN AGENT CAN HELP YOU
An agent will help you ensure that your proposal is as salable as it can be before submitting it. An agent is better able than a writer to judge the literary and commercial value of a proposal and to obtain the best possible editor, publisher and deal for a book. After a book is sold, the agent is the author's advocate with the publisher if questions arise during the publication of the book. An agent also pursues the sales of the subsidiary rights that the agent retains on the author's behalf.

QUERY LETTERS THAT GET RESULTS
It's been said that a query letter should be like a skirt: long enough to cover the subject but short enough to keep it interesting. In three or four paragraphs, describe the essence of your book, the markets for it and your background.

Use the information from the first part of your proposal, but change the wording so you won't diminish the impact of your proposal. Keep your letter to one page of single-spaced copy with easier-to-read indented paragraphs and spaces between the paragraphs.

Author Leon Fletcher believes that a letter is the fourth part of a proposal. Like the other three parts, each line must convince editors to read the next line.

Poor prose kills more query letters and proposals than anything else. Your query letter doesn't have to be funny or imaginative. But it creates the first and perhaps only impression agents or editors will have of you, so it must be impeccable. As an agent once said to us: "If they can't write a letter, they couldn't write a book."

Consider enclosing something simple but imaginative to catch an agent's or editor's attention. When she was submitting a book on assertiveness for women, AAR member Jillian Manus once enclosed a whip with a note attached to it saying: "Submit to your editor."

Large agencies and publishers are perpetually deluged with mail, phone calls and meetings, so they prefer to be queried by mail. But as long as you tell them, you may query as many of them as you wish simultaneously.

Clip a postage-paid self-addressed postcard with the agent's or editor's name and your return address on it to the front of the letter. On the back of the card, have just two lines of copy, one underneath the other:

_____ Please send the proposal.
_____ Sorry, we can't help.

No matter how busy they are, agents and editors interested in new writers will take the time to read a one-page letter and put a check mark on a postcard.

Your query letter and proposal are like direct-mail advertising. Agents and editors respond to form letters the same way you do. Individualize your letters. Agents and editors want to be wanted. If you can, tell them why you're approaching them. For more on query letters, please see my book on agents.

Send the proposal to those who respond positively. Once editors express interest in seeing your proposal, it is no longer unsolicited. You can make a multiple submission of your proposal, and it will not wind up in the dreaded slush pile. Indicate as you did in your query letter that it is a multiple submission. Start your cover letter with, "Many thanks for giving me the opportunity to send you my proposal for. . . ."

Find out how long it takes agents or editors to respond, make a note of the date by which they indicate you will have a response, and follow up by mail or phone if you don't.

If you receive an offer from one of them, give the others a week to respond. Better still, thank the publisher for the offer but don't discuss it, and seek help from an agent or a literary attorney who specializes in publishing.

> ⚡ **HOT TIP** In *A Writer's Guide to Book Publishing*, Richard Balkin recommends sending the proposal with the query letter to save time. If time is more important to you than money, and you're not concerned about agents or editors already working on competitive projects, do it.

ENTRUSTING YOUR FUTURE TO THE MAILS

Someone once defined a manuscript as "something submitted in haste and returned at leisure." For the best treatment at the receiving end, submit your proposal properly.

As agents and publishers do not assume responsibility for lost or damaged manuscripts, it behooves you to package your proposal carefully. Place the proposal in a manila envelope or, for greater protection, a no. 5 mailing bag.

In his book *How to Write Short Stories*, Ring Lardner warned: "A good many young writers make the mistake of enclosing a stamped, self-addressed envelope, big enough for the manuscript to come back in. This is too much of a temptation to the editor." Lardner may have a point, but agents and editors have no obligation to return submissions unless you provide them with the means to do so.

Always enclose a stamped, self-addressed mailer if you want the material returned. At this writing, packages weighing more than a pound must be brought to the post office, which may delay their return.

To avoid this, enclose a prepaid return label from another shipper like United Parcel Service or Federal Express. If you don't need the material back, say so. Just include a stamped, self-addressed no. 10 envelope to be sure of receiving a response. Five staples will seal a mailing bag effectively; avoid string or tape. The post office recommends that you tape the side of the staples with the points.

Naturally you want to be sure your proposal arrives. *Don't call!* Agents and editors hate wasting their time with "did-you-get-it?" calls. Use United Parcel Service, spring for a return receipt at the post office or clip a postcard to the front of your letter with your address filled in and the following message on the back:

We received (Title) on _____.
We will get back to you by _____.
Name _____.

If you don't use a postcard, find out by phone or by mail or from a directory listing how long the reading will take before you send your proposal. A six- to eight-week turnaround is typical for established agents. Publishers also vary in how quickly they process submissions, but they usually take longer than agents.

Once your proposal is accepted by a large house, allow two months for the contract to arrive and another two months for the advance. The amount of time will depend on the size and efficiency of the house, what else is going on in the house at the time and how complicated the deal is.

THE IDEAL REVIEW OF THIS BOOK (AND YOURS)

Before or after you start writing your proposal, take a break and have some fun. Set a literary goal for yourself by writing the ideal review of your book. You will have total freedom to give yourself a review that will make even you blush.

Then put it up on the wall where you write. Let it inspire you to do your best. Before you share your proposal with anyone, ask yourself: Could this proposal merit that review? If not, one of them needs revision.

You know it's time to submit your proposal when you think it deserves your review. Consider submitting the review at the end of your proposal. If an agent and an editor agree with you, you're on your way!

The Ideal Review of *How to Write a Book Proposal*
Literary agent Michael Larsen makes his living by using his book *How to Write a Book Proposal* to sell his clients' work. His book

does an excellent job of showing writers how they can make their living by following its clear instructions.

Larsen keeps the structure of a proposal admirably simple. He divides a proposal into three parts: an introduction that provides editors with fifteen kinds of information about the book and the author, a chapter-by-chapter outline and one or two sample chapters. He uses helpful examples throughout the book and includes three first-rate proposals at the end of the book.

Throughout the book, Larsen maintains an engaging balance between a realistic, proven approach to writing and selling proposals and a can-do inspirational tone that will keep you turning the pages. Just the hot tips he scatters throughout the book are worth more than what you will pay for it.

Larsen's upbeat approach will leave readers optimistic and eager to start on their books. In fact, the only problem I had is that when I finished reading his book, I couldn't resist starting one of my own!

How to Write a Book Proposal has already sold more than sixty thousand copies. This revised, state-of-the-art version will sell many more.

Larsen has been a literary agent in San Francsico for twenty-five years. During this time, he and his partner Elizabeth Pomada have written or coauthored thirteen books and sold books to more than one hundred publishers. Larsen is the author of *Literary Agents: What They Do, How They Do It, and How to Find and Work With the Right One for You*. He is a member of the Association of Authors Representatives.

When you are satisfied with your review, write down the advance you want for it at the top of the page. You have now established your literary and financial goals for your book. Now all you have to do is write a proposal that will achieve them!

THE LAST WORD

It is good to have an end to journey toward; but it is the journey that matters, in the end.
    —Science fiction author Ursula K. LeGuin

Every book is a book, yet every book is different, a unique combination of content, author, publisher and timing. Once you

HOT TIP This book can change your life. If you have a salable idea, prepare a proposal, and sell it, you will no longer be just a writer with an idea. You will be an author, as in authority, with a book to your credit.

You will have increased your writing skills, your understanding of publishing and promotion, and the number of professional contacts you know who can help you. All of these strengths will make you more valuable to your publisher because you will be a better writer and more able to help make your books successful.

As an author, you will be in a position to go from book to book and advance to advance, as long as you, your agent or your editor can come up with book ideas and you can write proposals and books based on them.

Practice nichecraft: Choose a subject that lends itself to a series of books that you will enjoy writing and promoting, and you can carve a career out of it.

To sustain your momentum, however, you must keep turning ideas into proposals. Unless you plan to continue researching your book while your completed proposal is being sold, go on to your next proposal immediately. Unless you need breathing room between books, aim to have the proposal for your next book arrive on the first day that your editor is willing to look at it.

Once you or your agent starts submitting your proposal, take one of three steps:

- If you need to, take a break to recharge your batteries.
- If you have enough faith that your proposal will sell, continue to research and write your book.
- If you have an idea, start your next proposal.

Since the proposal may not sell, don't waste time waiting for it to happen. You are also less likely to suffer postpartum depression after your baby leaves the nursery if you have another project in the works.

No matter how experienced a writer you are, a fantastic idea may hit you at any time. Be ready to take advantage of it!

set out on the journey to reach your literary goals, you must rely on your common sense and trust your instincts.

However arduous this approach to preparing a proposal may be, it's the fastest, easiest way we know to get the best possible editor, publisher and deal for your book, and for creating the best possible book. But only our clients have to follow it scrupulously. Feel free to use the suggestions in the book in whatever way works best for you and your book.

A final suggestion: For the best results, use this book in conjunction with the last four chapters of my book on agents. They contain information about writing, publishing, developing your carft and making a commitment to your career that you need to know before approaching an agent or publisher.

You may have to write a proposal as thorough as this only once in your life. I guarantee you that if you have a salable idea, write an excellent proposal, and you or your agent present it to the right editor at the right publisher at the right time, you will sell it. Good luck!

CHECK THESE SIX SOURCES
TO FIND COMPETITIVE BOOKS

- **Bookstores.** Two of the joys of the literary life are browsing in bookstores and buying books. Become friends with booksellers who love books. Buying books and discussing your favorites is all you have to do.

Booksellers thrive on their passion for good books, and they light up when they find a kindred spirit with whom they can share their latest discovery. Someday, they will stock your book and have a book-signing party for you.

At this writing, Amazon.com has become a handy alternative to *BIP*. An online bookstore, Amazon lists more than two million books. The number of bookstores online is growing, so you can let your fingertips do the walking and investigate the alternatives as well.

 HOT TIP Ask your local or online bookseller to send you or notify you about new books on your subject.

- **Books in Print (BIP).** *BIP* is an annual compilation that lists all books in print three ways: by title, author and subject. The subject guide in BIP or in an online bookstore will tell you what's available on the subject you're writing about. For children's books, read *Children's Books in Print*. Online bookstores have up-to-date listings.
- **Forthcoming Books.** Issued bimonthly, *Forthcoming Books* lists the books announced since the latest edition of *BIP*.
- **Publishers Weekly.** This weekly trade journal reviews upcoming books and publishes spring, summer and fall announcement issues in which publishers list their new titles.
- **Publisher's Trade List Annual (PTLA).** The *PTLA* lists books by publisher so you can see which publishers are most interested in your subject. Reading the catalogs of those publishers will enable you to get a feel for the lists of different publishers.
- **Bibliographies of competitive books.**

APPENDIX 2
THREE SAMPLE PROPOSALS

Here are three excellent proposals. They are annotated as needed. The first is for what was finally called *When Life Becomes Precious: A Guide for Loved Ones and Friends of Cancer Patients*. Please follow the formatting instructions in the book that space limitations prevented us from following here.

A Proposal for
When Life Becomes Precious, You Need More Than Flowers:
A Comprehensive Guide for Friends, Loved Ones
and Co-workers of Cancer Patients
By Elise NeeDell Babcock

Table of Contents

[Elise starts her proposal with a long but effective anecdote, before her equally effective subject and book hooks.]

Introduction
Overview

Anna was the kind of girl that people noticed. Her huge brown trusting eyes were almost as striking as her waist-length tendrils of twisting hair. Her fifteen-year-old wit charmed everyone, but no one appreciated her like Jeremy. He adored his daughter. Yet when he got cancer, the laughter, the talking, the long evenings they spent together, came to an end.

He never told her why his eyes were surrounded by sunken lines, why his bones protruded from his too-thin arms or why he spent his nights and many of his days, curled beneath his covers, behind walls Anna did not understand. She was left alone to imagine why her father no longer wanted her.

Looking back, his very private wife Nancy, pondered her role in what was to happen next. "I suppose I should have told Anna about her father. I was so caught up in my own grief, my own shock, I couldn't talk to anyone about this disease, especially her."

Jeremy recovered. Anna did not. Two years after vigorous treatments, the cancer was gone. Anna was pregnant, drinking heavily and climbing out her bedroom window. Sometimes she'd leave for weeks. After giving birth to Tim, Anna climbed out that window one last time, leaving her parents to raise her son.

Fifteen years later, Jeremy's cancer was back. Until then, Tim was, "A good boy," said Nancy, "never a bit of trouble. A football player with above-average grades, and he had such nice friends."

Two months into Jeremy's chemotherapy, Tim started climbing out the same window his mother had. His grades dropped. The nice friends disappeared. Nancy discovered drugs in his room. Still she and Jeremy thought they could handle Tim, until he almost died of an overdose.

Jeremy and Nancy decided they weren't going to lose another child. They joined a weekly support group for couples coping with cancer. The author and a psychiatrist led these groups. They taught Jeremy and Nancy the principles that the author will reveal in her book.

Five months after joining the group, Nancy wrote, "Tim is getting all As and Bs. He's drug free. After following your advice, we also wrote Anna, telling her all those things we never knew how to before.

"We are better parents now and closer as a couple. You have helped us to prevent the past from repeating itself. We can't change what happened with Anna, but we have changed the way we raise Tim.

"Then last week as I was fixing dinner, someone knocked at our door. No one ever visits us unannounced. I expected to see someone who had lost his way.

"There she stood, twisting a tendril of her dark wavy hair, those piercing eyes smiling up at me. I pulled Anna in and I cried, tears I never even knew I had. As I held her, I could see Tim. Without a word, he leaped towards the door, scooping us off our feet, encircling Anna and me, in his arms.

"As I write this, I can hear Anna, Jeremy and Tim, laughing in the other room. I know all too well what pain this disease brings, but you taught us how we could turn our tragedy into an opportunity to bring our daughter home."

"You have cancer."

Eight million people like Jeremy began 1995 having heard those words. Another one million will hear them before the year is over. Experts predict those numbers will continue to increase.

The emotional impact of the illness on patients is enormous. The disease is also devastating to those who watch people they care about endure months of medical treatments.

If each of these nine million patients has just five people who care about them, there are forty-five million friends, relatives and co-workers of cancer patients in this country alone. Since all Americans will be affected by cancer in their lifetime, either as patients or loved ones, the number will go well beyond forty-five million.

Using her twenty-one years of personal and professional experience, the author will give readers the vital tools they need to take care of themselves, while they take care of their loved ones. *When Life Becomes Precious, You Need More Than Flowers: A Comprehensive Guide for Friends, Loved Ones and Co-workers of Cancer Patients* will be the ultimate handbook for this growing population.

When Life Becomes Precious will be the first book to:

- offer 150 tips on ways to help patients, caregivers and co-workers
- provide the longest list ever compiled of gifts to give to families living with cancer
- give ten reasons why people avoid talking about it
- present the eight things families do that drive doctors crazy and seven they appreciate.

The manuscript will be 69,000 words, and it will have twelve cartoons and fifteen pages of back matter. The book will be divided into five sections, each of which will cover an issue related to the most common questions asked by loved ones, co-workers and friends of patients.

Readers who follow the author's tips and principles will be better equipped to not only live with cancer, but to grow from it. *When Life Becomes Precious* will illustrate these principles with anecdotes, exercises, question-and-answer sections and tips. The principles can be used regardless of the reader's age or the stage of the patient's disease.

When readers finish *When Life Becomes Precious*, they will

understand how their most painful experiences can also be their most rewarding. They will approach cancer as an opportunity to change their lives in ways they never imagined, fulfilling dreams they never thought possible, making each day, each moment more precious.

When Life Becomes Precious will go right to the heart of the problems its readers are facing. The author will teach them how to develop realistic hopes they can live by, faith they can count on and the powerful communication tools they will need to survive. The book will become a timeless inspirational guide, a moving testimonial to the resilience of the human spirit.

The book will include advice from world-renowned experts:
- Dr. Jimmie Holland, chief of psychiatry, Memorial Sloan Kettering
- Dr. Charles A. LeMaistre, president, Houston's M.D. Anderson Cancer Center, the largest cancer center in the world; and 1986 president of The American Cancer Society
- Dr. Eugene Carlton, president, American Board of Urology
- Dr. Lamar McGinnis, president, the American Cancer Society
- Dr. Stratton C. Hill, founder of the pain-control movement and the chairman of M.D. Anderson's Pain Center

It will have inspirational stories and advice from:
- Dr. Steve Allen Jr., motivational speaker
- Dave Dravecky, author and former Giants' pitcher
- Bill Martin, *My Prostrate & Me* (Multimedia, 1994)
- Families the author worked with as the leader of the first agency in the nation to provide professional counseling for cancer patients and their families during all stages of the disease

The book will offer a candid look into the lives of families living with cancer, each of whom had to learn how to survive in the face of adversity. Their stories will show how courage and humor can carry people through unimaginable circumstances.

Back matter
The back will include a thirteen-page resource section and a two-page bibliography.

[I recommend using shorthand for a title so that after editors have read it, writers don't slow them down by making them keep reading the whole title. Elise's title doesn't lend itself to shortening, but it's only four words.]

Markets for the book

Besides the forty-five million loved ones, potential markets include over 450,000 medical and nursing students and professionals who work with cancer patients and their families. The advice in the book is also applicable for loved ones and friends in more than twenty foreign markets.

A relatively new market is the nationwide volunteer force that has grown in the past ten years. More than six million volunteers work for hospices, social service agencies, self-help groups and hospitals. The book is exactly what teachers need for volunteer training programs.

The 1980s take-charge-get-educated approach to illness has paved the way for books on coping with cancer. More than 350,000 people bought *Love, Medicine and Miracles* (Harper & Row, 1986). Since then, the popularity and backlist sales of his books for patients prove the need for a book for their loved ones.

Love, Medicine and Miracles was on the best-seller list for fifty-three weeks. The market for books about the emotional impact of cancer has exploded since then. Loved ones have gone from not being able to say the word "cancer" to reading everything they can find on the topic. While books for patients continue to be published, the market of loved ones and friends grows larger.

When Life Becomes Precious will have long-term appeal because readers can turn to the book as a reference guide the very first day they hear about the diagnosis and again three years later when it's time for the annual checkup. The same reader will use the book over and over, reading it page-by-page one day and skimming through it another.

Spin-offs

The author plans to write three books that will help sell *When Life Becomes Precious*:

1. *Making Life More Precious.* At the end of the book, the author will ask readers for suggestions and stories. The next book will use these and additional interviews to expand on the tips and suggestions of the first book.

2. *Who's Laughing Now?* This will be a collection of jokes and humorous stories for cancer patients and their loved ones.

3. *Controlling Megan, a novel.* While her husband is fighting for his life, Megan comes face to face with a past that she can no longer control. As her husband conquers cancer, Megan must decide if she can give up control to prevent the destruction of her marriage.

[Elise's promotion plan is at the end of the proposal. Because her book faced no competition yet many books had been written on the subject, Elise used the competitive books section to show how, because of her experience and the idea for the book, her book would be unique.]

Competitive books

More than one million Americans will be diagnosed with cancer this year. Only 15 percent of these are breast cancer patients. The other 85 percent have prostate, lung, colon and other types of cancer. Yet 90 percent of the books on the market are for breast cancer patients and their families.

The three national organizations—National Cancer Institute, American Cancer Society and the National Coalition for Cancer Survivorship—recommend twenty-three books for breast cancer and only seven other books. When the author and the manager of a Barnes & Noble store reviewed *Books in Print*, they found 275 books under cancer. Five addressed the unique issues that families face. The manager had only recommended one of these books.

The outstanding books on death and dying already do a superb job at covering grief-related issues. The works of Elizabeth Kubler-Ross, June Cerza Kolf and Harriet Sarnott Schiff are as popular today as they were in the 1980s.

Books about alternative care or one person's cancer experience help patients but most of these books are often too long, graphic, offbeat, technical or otherwise difficult to read for loved ones and friends. The excellent medical books are used for technical data, not for information on the psychological impact of the disease.

The existing books for loved ones and friends focused on one person's experience. None of the writers addresses the emotional issues associated with all stages of the disease. These books skim the topics that the author's personal and professional experience enable her to cover in depth.

The author is incorporating information from her participation in the most up-to-date training of medical personnel. She also shares her experiences as founder and president of a cancer organization and talks about her work as a co-leader with a Columbia University-trained psychiatrist of the nation's first support groups for couples coping with cancer. During weekly sessions, members explored every issue that affected their lives.

Few people can have the information that comes from a career of listening to the issues, questions and problems of so many people from so many different backgrounds. However, information is not enough. The author has used her experiences to write brochures that have taught thousands of people how to help cancer patients and their families.

Books for cancer patients, medical books and books on death and dying, complement *When Life Becomes Precious*, but they cannot take the place of it. While the patients are reading books designed for them, friends, co-workers and loved ones will now have their own comprehensive guide written by an expert in the field.

[As time was the only resource that Elise needed to write her book, her proposal didn't require a separate page for resources.]

The manuscript will be ready six months after the receipt of the advance. The manuscript will be available in Microsoft Word 6.0.

[Elise's bio shows how well qualified she is to write her book.]

About the Author

Elise NeeDell Babcock is the founder of Cancer Counseling, of Houston, Texas, the first agency in the country to provide professional counseling to cancer patients and their families during any stage of the disease.

Since 1974, she has lectured, trained and provided consulting and counseling services to more than ninety thousand people. Her written materials and interviews have reached more than five million people.

She started the nation's first support groups for couples coping with cancer, children of cancer patients and widow and widowers with young children.

She served as president (1982-1994) and chairman (1982-1990) of Cancer Counseling and is a member of the Board of Directors. She is a consultant to the Texas Cancer Council. In 1994, she helped lead a weekly support group for foreigners and out-of-state families for M.D. Anderson Cancer Center.

At Cancer Counseling, Babcock recruited and supervised a staff of twenty therapists, including psychologists, social workers and psychiatrists. She had over 350 volunteers, including leaders of Fortune 500 companies, internationally known doctors and the Houston Rockets basketball players.

She wrote all of her agency's educational, fund-raising and media materials, including 210 press releases, thirty-three press kits, 110 newsletters, twelve annual reports and six brochures. She raised more than two million dollars.

The most popular of her materials was *I Have Cancer, This Is What You Can Do*, a brochure she wrote with two of her patients. It has a worldwide distribution of 770,000 reprints and copies. Every major cancer center, *Coping* magazine and companies across the country have reprinted the brochure.

Coping with Cancer in the Workplace, a brochure being revised for the author's book, was reprinted by the *Houston Chronicle* and the Houston Chamber of Commerce. UPI and fifty publications have featured stories about the author and Cancer Counseling.

Besides having appeared on every Houston television and radio station, Babcock recruited anchors from CBS, NBC and ABC affiliates to host her fund-raising events.

The publisher, society editor and lifestyle editor of the *Houston Chronicle* also hosted fund-raisers. In 1984, the author was one of seven Houstonians to give tips on "Secrets for Happiness" for the *Chronicle*'s Christmas edition.

Babcock has extensive experience providing presentations and training seminars for hospitals, nursing and medical associations, social service agencies, women's groups, corporate and civic groups.

She began working with cancer patients in 1974 as a volunteer at John Runnels Hospital in New Jersey. After receiving her B.A. from Florida Atlantic University in 1980, Babcock attended weekly psychiatry-oncology rounds for two years at the University of Miami Medical School, five years of weekly cancer conferences at Baylor College of Medicine and numerous other cancer and writers' conferences and Dale Carnegie courses.

In 1993, M.D. Anderson Cancer Center honored Babcock for being a partner in the fight against cancer. She has appeared in *Who's Who of American Women, 17th edition*, 1991-1992, *Who's Who of American Young Professionals, 2nd edition*, 1992-1993, *Who's Who in the World, 11th edition*, 1993-1994, and *Two Thousand Notable American Women, 6th edition*.

Babcock is a member of the National Writer's Association, The National Writer's Union, Sisters in Crime, The Women's Research and Education Fund, The National Coalition for Cancer Survivorship and The International Platform Association.

She lives in Houston, Texas, with her husband, Jack, and her newborn daughter, Megan (Lexi) Alexandra.

[This double-spaced list begins on a new page.]

The Outline
List of Chapters

PART I: What You May Be Feeling and What to Do About It
  Chapter 1   The Five Common Reactions:
               How to Assess Your Feelings When Cancer Strikes
  Chapter 2   Why You Can't Talk About It:
               How to Overcome the Ten Most Common Fears

PART II: What You Can Do: 101 Tips and 67 Gifts for Helping
          Patients, Primary Caregivers, Children and Co-Workers
  Chapter 3   What Do You Say? What Do You Do?:
               26 Guidelines to Successful Support
  Chapter 4   More Guidelines for Giving: 26 Tips You Can Use
  Chapter 5   Supporting Primary Caregivers:
               14 Ways You Can Help
  Chapter 6   How to Manage Cancer in the Workplace:
               18 Techniques To Take Care of Your Employees
  Chapter 7   40 Things You Should Know About Helping
               Children Live With a Parent's Cancer
  Chapter 8   From the Goodness of Your Heart:
               67 Gifts You Can Give

PART III: Become A Partner With Those Who Can Help You
  Chapter 9   How to Master the Medical Maze:
               Building and Coaching a Winning Health-Care
               Team
  Chapter 10   A Lifeline You Shouldn't Be Without:
               How Counseling Can Help You

PART IV: Charting Your Way Through Cancer
  Chapter 11   Giving Without Giving Out
  Chapter 12   Making Life Work Anyway:
               How to Plan the "Just-in-Case" Lifestyle
  Chapter 13   God Has Big Shoulders:
               Developing Faith You Can Count On

PART V: The Continuing Challenges

Chapter 14   Making Merry Holidays:
               The Twelve Keys to Stress-Free Celebrations

[We have included the outline for chapter two as a sample.]

Chapter Two

Why You Can't Talk About It:
How to Overcome the Ten Most Common Fears   24 Pages

The author presents the ten most common reasons people don't
reach out the minute they hear someone has cancer. She also shows
readers how it's possible to speak to someone every day, but when
cancer enters the picture, the rules suddenly change. Loved ones and
friends no longer know what to do or say.

By evaluating the reasons why they avoid the subject, readers will
be able to overcome their fears. Each reason is followed by a story
or analysis. The reasons are:

1. I'm afraid of saying the wrong thing.
2. I think I should wait to call until after the surgery.
3. I'm afraid to rock the boat.
4. I feel unprepared to talk about cancer.
5. I'm afraid we won't have anything to say to each other.
6. Hearing about cancer reminds me of another friend or family
   member's cancer.
7. It makes me realize how vulnerable I am.
8. We're not that close.
9. I'm afraid I will get in over my head.
10. I'm afraid the person will cry, and I just don't know how to
    deal with tears.

The author continues this discussion by giving readers three questions to analyze:
"What else could I be afraid of?"
"What is the worst thing that could happen if I discuss my
feelings?"
"Do I have unresolved issues with the person?"
The last section of the chapter shows readers how to make that
first call or talk about the cancer in spite of their fears. However,
the author points out that it may be more appropriate for some
people to write a note or give a gift if they are still not ready to talk
with the person.

[Elise NeeDell Babcock wrote one of the strongest promotion plans that we have seen. Elise divided her plan into two parts: one on publication and a lifetime plan. Elise began her plan with a title page and its own table of contents on separate pages. Because the plan was ten pages, we placed it in the left pocket of a paper folder.]

A Promotion Plan for
When Life Becomes Precious, You Need More Than Flowers:
A Comprehensive Guide for Friends, Loved Ones
and Co-workers of Cancer Patients
and
A Lifetime Promotion Plan
for the Author's Cancer Books

Table of Contents

Promotion

The author is committed to writing and promoting books that improve the lives of cancer patients and their families. Her writing and marketing skills give her the solid background needed to make every book she writes a best-seller.

The author is applying the same principles, energy and determination to promotion as Jack Canfield did for his *Chicken Soup* books. She is hiring Canfield's publicist for radio and television interviews and will use her existing relationships to develop nationwide corporate, medical and media contacts.

The author will obtain endorsements from the people interviewed for the book, Barbara Taylor Bradford and Jack Canfield. Friends of the author are contacting the following for endorsements: Stephen Covey, George Foreman, Beverly Sills, Barbara Bush and Colin Powell.

The author will match the publisher's consumer promotion budget up to $____, and she will buy ____ copies of the book. During the first six months of her campaign, the author will:

• Set up a publicity tour to Boston, Dallas, Atlanta, Miami, Los Angeles, San Diego, San Francisco, New York, Washington, DC,

Philadelphia, Seattle, Denver, Cleveland, Minneapolis and Milwaukee.

• Retain Rick Frishman of Planned Television Arts to schedule one-hour radio interviews, to produce a satellite television tour and to schedule national talk show interviews.

• Contract with Metro Creative Graphics to produce camera-ready feature stories and distribute them to lifestyle, business and health editors at the nation's two hundred leading newspapers, including *The Houston Business Journal*, *The Wall Street Journal*, *The New York Times* and *The Washington Post*. Each department will receive a story with a different angle.

• Schedule interviews and send press kits to the Houston media to reach their audience of four million people. A *Houston Chronicle* columnist has already announced the author is writing the book to the paper's one million readers.

Brochures

• Print fifteen thousand three-fold brochures containing twelve of the book's tips, a copy of the book jacket and the author's 800 number: (800) 547-LEXI. Brochures will also be used as a tool to generate interest in the media and the author's contacts. The first printing of the brochure will be distributed as follows:

10,000 to the seven comprehensive care centers
150 to health-care agencies
700 to the author's contacts in corporations and civic groups
the remainder to the media, booksellers and librarians

Press kits, promotional video and new releases

• The author will develop individualized press kits, a five-minute video and news releases for the media, corporations, civic groups and health-care organizations.

• She will send press releases and brochures to smaller papers and radio stations.

Promotional copies

The author will use fifteen hundred promotional copies for the following:

• Seven hundred leading oncologists in Houston, West Palm Beach, Miami, Los Angeles, San Diego, San Francisco, Washington, DC, Boston and New York for their waiting rooms.

- Forty professors who are interested in incorporating the book into their training programs for graduate students in nursing, medicine, social work and psychology.
- Forty-five people who have an interest in having the author present workshops for their civic groups, corporations and women's organizations.
- Thirty-one representatives of the Houston media who will do stories, an Associated Press reporter who has requested an interview with the author and her agency.
- The remainder will go to the educational departments of the seven comprehensive care centers, eleven major cancer hospitals, the twenty largest Cancer Information Services (CIS), the twenty top American Cancer Society offices, The National Coalition for Cancer Survivorship and the Komen Foundation in Dallas.

Conferences
- Promote the book at conferences by buying booths and conducting workshops. More than two hundred health-care leaders and seven hundred families attend each conference. After meeting the author, leaders will promote the book to their volunteers, employees and patients. They can reach more than six million people who will have an interest in the book. Conferences include:

M.D. Anderson's National Cancer Conference
National Coalition for Cancer Survivorship
The American Psychological Association
American Academy of Nursing
American Family Therapy Association
American Society of Clinical Oncology.

- Send a news release about the book to fifteen hundred of the author's contacts.
- Provide promotional copies of the book to human relations departments of companies who have supported Cancer Counseling. She will send the chapter on "Managing Cancer in the Workplace" to their employee publications which have previously published her stories, including Shell, Exxon, Conoco and Mobil.
- Send promotional copies of the book to two hundred physicians and hospitals for waiting rooms.
- Offer to be a guest speaker online for Prodigy, America Online and CompuServe.

- Send promotional copies of the book to 150 health-care organizations and hospitals with whom she has established long-term
working relationships. She has interviewed leaders of twenty-one of
these organizations for the book.

Ads

- Buy three half-page ads in *Coping*, the only national cancer
magazine. *Coping* has 280,000 readers and has previously devoted
a page to the author's brochure. They will write a story when the
book is published.
- Buy a half-page ad in *USA Today*.

First serial rights and excerpts

- Contact the top magazines about first serial rights in the fol-
lowing areas: General Interest, Women, Health, Business, Parenting
and Men. These include: *Family Circle Magazine*, *Woman's Day*,
Redbook Magazine, *Good Housekeeping*, *Ladies' Home Journal*,
Today's Health, *Parents Magazine*, *Child*, *Prevention* and *Reader's
Digest*.
- Provide excerpts of the book to human relations departments
of companies for their employee publications which have previously
published her stories, including Shell, Exxon, Conoco and Mobil.
- Send excerpts of the book to 150 health-care organizations
with whom she has established long-term working relationships.
These organizations, which reach more than eight million people
each year, will use the book for their training programs and include
excerpts of the book in their newsletters.

The three largest agencies are:

1. The American Cancer Society. The 1986 and 1995 presidents and a Regional Volunteer Coordinator are quoted in
   the book. ACS has four million volunteers.
2. Cancer Information Service (1-800-4-Cancer in all states),
   a division of the National Cancer Institute. This nationwide
   800 number receives more than 500,000 calls from cancer
   patients and their families each year.
3. The director of the M.D. Anderson Network will include a
   one-page excerpt of the book in the center's newsletter
   which has a worldwide readership of seventy thousand
   people.

- Send excerpts from the book to cancer centers which have

printed or distributed the author's previous brochures, including Johns Hopkins Oncology Center, Dana-Farber Cancer Institute and Mayo Comprehensive Cancer Center.

  • Cancer Counseling will print excerpts of the book in its newsletter, which has a readership of fifteen thousand, and it will promote the book at its annual conference.

Gift shops and gift trade fairs
The author will meet with hospital and health-care gift shop managers and attend gift trade fairs to promote her book.

Online discussions
Offer to be a guest speaker online for Prodigy, America Online and CompuServe.

Speakers' bureaus
Hire speakers' bureaus.

QVC and home shopping networks
The author will solicit these networks for promotional time.

National Infomercial meetings
The author will attend NIMA's annual meeting to obtain an infomercial sponsor.

[Elise's Lifetime Marketing Plan was on a separate page.]

Lifetime Marketing Plan
The author plans on continuing to market her books by:
  • scheduling forty radio shows a month
  • scheduling three presentations a month to companies, civic groups, conferences or health-care workers
  • updating and distributing brochures (with excerpt of the book) to hospitals, corporations, health-care agencies and medical, nursing and graduate schools
  • maintaining the 800-number
  • participating in health-care conferences and fairs by providing workshops, brochures and purchasing booths
  • developing a newsletter and starting a syndicated column
  • providing seminars for Learning Annex and bookstores
  • advertising in newspapers
  • identifying and exploiting market niches
  • scheduling annual visits to the comprehensive care centers and

the American Cancer Society offices for presentations to the
staff of their 800 services

• submitting excerpts to magazines, newspapers and health-care
organizations.

[P.S. While we were at the Maui Writers Conference, I suggested that Elise talk to Toni Burbank, excutive editor at Bantam Books, about her book. After Toni read Elise's proposal, Toni became her editor.

Elise's six-figure advance, how well the book turned out, and what a tireless promoter Elise is all helped make this book memorable, but nothing was dearer to us than how kind Elise was to us in her acknowledgments.]

[What became *Your Next Fifty Years: A Completely New Way to Look at How, When, and If You Should Retire* was Ginita Wall's fourth book, and her third with Theresa Burns at Henry Holt. It was also Victoria Collins's third book. No sample chapter was required. The ladies' previous book was their first collaboration. Faith Popcorn would agree that a book about retiring baby boomers was "on trend."]

A Proposal for
Your Next Fifty Years:
Smart Retirement Strategies for Baby Boomers
By Ginita Wall, CPA, CFP and
Victoria F. Collins, Ph.D., CFP

Table of Contents

[Is seventy-six million potential readers a big enough market? You betcha. Enough said, even with the inevitable competition. There can never be too many books for a market that huge, especially on a subject so vital. I recommend that writers avoid asking editors questions. But the authors use them well, and answer them immediately.]

Introduction
Overview

In 1996, four million baby boomers turn fifty, and seventy-three million more boomers will turn fifty in the years that follow. A whole generation of individuals passing the half-century mark is an event that demands a new perspective on retirement.

• Are the boomers ready for retirement? It's doubtful—the baby-boom generation has the poorest savings record of any single generation, and fewer corporate pensions provided and funded by corporations.

• Are the boomers concerned about retirement? According to a major study done by the International Association for Financial

Planning, the number one financial concern of Americans today is retirement planning.

• Do baby boomers really need a retirement guide just for them? Yes—unfortunately the old tried-and-true retirement planning doesn't address baby boomers' concerns. They've saved little, spent a lot, divorced and remarried, seen pensions cut and social security squeezed, and they will live longer than any generation ever has.

These facts alone not only make retirement planning more complex but also call into question everything about retirement in the traditional sense, as baby boomers decide whether the conventional concept of retirement is relevant to them.

In addition, many are caught in the "Sandwich Generation" triple squeeze—they must plan for their own retirement at the same time they are educating children and helping care for their aging parents.

Over ten trillion dollars will pass into the hands of the baby boomers over the next fifty years—the largest inter-generational transfer of wealth ever—but it won't be enough, or come soon enough. Because the aging baby boomers are concerned, they are ripe for retirement planning.

[Ginita and Victoria know that any trend this large will attract a host of competitive books. So they did a good job of setting their book off from the competition.]

Your Next Fifty Years: Smart Retirement Strategies for Baby Boomers will be the first retirement guide to:

• focus on the psychological as well as the financial impediments to planning for retirement
• allow readers to tailor a financial plan unique to them
• suggest alternatives to the traditional concept of retirement, such as sabbaticals, flextime and temporary or partial retirement
• challenge readers to develop a lifelong approach to planning (as opposed to planning for retirement as an event)
• alert readers to the subtleties that occur when finances and feelings collide in planning for the years ahead
• provide a new perspective on retirement as a renaissance—not the end of working life, but rather a rebirth that provides a time to expand on the best of what readers have experienced
• provide twenty-four worksheets to guide readers.

The finished manuscript will contain 269 pages, including five pages of back matter.

[In addition to their track records and a timely idea, another of the strengths of this proposal is the authors' credentials. The authors emphasized their ability to write the book by placing their credentials right after the book hook.]

The authors of *Your Next Fifty Years* offer a unique combination of expertise. Ginita Wall, a Certified Financial Planner who is also a CPA, is joined by Victoria F. Collins, a Certified Financial Planner with a doctorate in psychology. Together, they present a new look at retirement planning.

The book is solid in financial advice and friendly in format. The readers of this book will be able to apply practical, topical and timely recommendations to their circumstances.

Icons and graphics will guide readers to information most relevant to them. This structure will set the book apart from its competition.

[They're thinking visually, a positive signal to editors. Visual appeal is needed all the more in a book of heavy-duty financial advice to add eye appeal.]

The book will be peppered with quotes of wisdom and useful sidebar information. It will include a variety of worksheets, questionnaires, charts and checklists. Back matter will include a three-page bibliography of books, periodicals and retirement planning software, and a two-page guide to agencies and organizations.

Although there are many books about retirement planning on the market, none focuses foremost on the unique retirement problems of the baby-boom generation in a psychologically motivating manner. This book will be upbeat, motivating readers to take immediate action.

Markets for the book

Your Next Fifty Years will appeal to people between the ages of thirty and fifty-five who seek a simple program for retirement planning. There are seventy-seven million people in this age group, and 64 percent of all households have discretionary income, so millions of them will be able to save for retirement. A special chapter of this book is devoted to the special retirement needs of women, who participate in 83 percent of all saving and investing decisions and who head more than ten million households.

Promotion

Ginita Wall and Victoria Collins have extensive media experience and are well-known lecturers, writers and experts in their respective fields. They will undertake a five-part promotion campaign for the book with the following components:

1. *Media campaign targeted to existing and new contacts*. The authors will develop a media campaign with the publisher to introduce the book to an extensive list of contacts developed through the publication of their prior books and subsequent interviews on a variety of financial planning topics.

The authors expect that the four hundred feature writers, journalists and TV and radio producers who know the authors will be interested in doing interviews about the book.

2. *Development, marketing and presentation of seminars based on the book*. The authors plan to create a seminar series using slides, graphics and examples based on the book to be presented in cities throughout the country. Venues for presentation will include (in order of potential for book sales):

- corporate-sponsored employee educational meetings and conventions
- community educational institutions such as the Learning Annex, university extension programs and local community college programs
- affinity groups such as AARP (American Association of Retired Persons), the Association of Realtors, the American Association of University Women, the Women's Institute for Financial Education and others
- professional organizations such as the International Association for Financial Planning, the National Association of Women Business Owners, the American Society of Women Accountants, CPA Clubs of America, Young Presidents' Organization and others.

3. *Speaking engagements to professional organizations, affinity groups and corporate employee programs*. The authors will continue to lecture regularly at national and regional meetings and conventions of the American Institute of CPAs, the College for Financial

Planning, International Association for Financial Planning, the American Women's Society of Certified Public Accountants and various CPA societies as well as corporate-sponsored engagements throughout the country. They will conduct television, radio and newspaper interviews in each city to which they travel individually.

Authors will also use their contacts in corporations for whom they have previously lectured such as the U.S. Post Office, Wells Fargo Bank, Downey Savings, IBM, the Hotel Institute, Chambers of Commerce and others.

The seminars—with accompanying book—are ideal for large corporations which sponsor employee seminars and conventions. Educational seminars on retirement planning have become big business as corporations downsize and shift the responsibility for investing and saving for retirement to employees.

4. *Sponsored seminars with banks, trust companies, mutual funds and other financial institutions.* Major financial institutions such as brokerage houses, banks and trust institutions are recognizing the growing need for retirement planning information for their retail consumers. They will also be a target market for the informational seminar developed by the authors.

If the publisher will supply books, the authors will send press kits to the following companies urging them to sponsor retirement planning seminars and create premium editions of the book to be distributed:

Banks. Since banks are aggressively seeking ways to attract and retain customers, the authors will contact directors of the marketing departments of the nation's twenty-five largest banks. Authors have already established relationships with Wells Fargo Bank and Citibank for whom they have lectured and written articles.

Mutual fund companies. The authors will contact the marketing departments of nineteen mutual fund companies, including Putnam for whom Ginita Wall has lectured. The baby-boom generation with its need for retirement investments is a primary target for mutual fund companies.

Brokerage firms. Ms. Wall has lectured for Prudential Securities and Merrill Lynch, and Dr. Collins does extensive work with Charles Schwab, the nation's largest discount broker. In addition to these major houses, the authors will contact the marketing departments of seven additional brokerage firms.

The authors will sell x thousand books a year.

5. *A tour*. Since both authors have extensive media experience and contacts, a tour using them individually will get twice the play. This tour will include Los Angeles, San Francisco, San Diego, Portland, Seattle, Phoenix, Tucson, Albuquerque, El Paso, Denver, Dallas, Houston, Austin, New Orleans, Atlanta, Miami, Baltimore, Philadelphia, Pittsburgh, Chicago, Washington, DC, New York, Hartford and Boston.

Competitive books

The competing books on retirement planning don't provide practical advice on all the financial aspects of retirement. They either focus on one particular aspect of retirement planning, such as investing or retirement plans, or else are very general.

None of the books address the psychological issues that are intertwined with the financial issues, and none of them offer alternatives to traditional concepts of retirement, such as semi-retirement and cyclical retirement.

Competing books published recently include:

Vanguard Retirement Investing Guide by the Vanguard Group (Irwin, 1995, $15.00). Focuses primarily on investing prior to and during retirement. Offers only two worksheets, and does not discuss psychological aspects or provide the reader a simple guide to creating a personalized retirement plan.

Don't Work Forever: Simple Steps Baby Boomers Must Take to Ever Retire by Steven G. Vernon (John Wiley & Sons, 1995, $14.95). Written very glibly, with references to the Beatles and the Stones and quotes from the Beatles. Has only two worksheets. Presents only traditional retirement concepts with no new perspectives.

Retirement Angles: 1001 Ways to Make Your Life Better Today and Tomorrow by Donald Jay Korn (Shot Tower Books, 1994, $15.95). Written in checklist form. Not cohesive. Not motivating and doesn't entice the reader to continue. Only three worksheets, and the investment section isn't comprehensive.

Making Up for Lost Time: Speed Investing for a Secure Future by Adriane Berg (Hearst Books, 1994, $22.00). Aimed at both retirement planning and planning for a child's education. Written in a down-to-earth, straightforward style, but with no integration of the psychological aspects of retirement. No worksheets.

Secure Your Future: Financial Planning at Any Age by Chuck D. Tellalian and Walter K. Rosen (Oasis Press, 1994, $19.95). Written by an insurance broker and a lawyer. Text sometimes too technical for the average reader. Has only three worksheets. Investment advice not its strength. Heavily slanted toward insurance products. Covers estate planning well, but too much of this short book devoted to it.

[No summary of why their book is different and better than the competition, because the authors had listed the seven elements that their book would be the first to provide.]

The manuscript will be delivered four months after receipt of the advance.

[After two books with her editor at Holt, Ginita didn't need a bio. But the other people in the house who have a say on the proposal didn't know Ginita as well, and the editorial board may have included new faces.]

About the Author

Ginita Wall, CPA, CFP is author of three previous books: *Our Money, Our Selves: Money Management for Each Stage of a Woman's Life* (Consumer Reports Books, 1992), *The Way to Save: A Ten-Step Blueprint for Lifetime Security* (Holt, 1994) and *The Way to Invest: A Five-Step Blueprint for Investing In Mutual Funds With As Little As $50 a Month* (Holt, 1995).

In addition, she has co-authored *Smart Ways to Save Money During and After Divorce* with Victoria F. Collins (Nolo Press, 1994) and *Cover Your Assets* with Jay Mitton (Crown Books, 1995). She is also author of two manuals for continuing education courses for CPAs.

Ginita lectures on mutual funds and other financial issues to accountants, financial professionals and general audiences across the country.

Sponsors of her lectures include Wells Fargo Bank, Merrill Lynch, Prudential Securities, E.F. Hutton, the International Association for Financial Planning, the American Institute of CPAs, the National Association for Financial Education, various state CPA societies, CPA Clubs of American Society of Women Accountants, Estate Planning Councils, the U.S. Post Office, the Learning Annex, university extension programs and many others.

The author has appeared on CBS Television's *This Morning*, Discovery Channel's *Home Matters*, National Public Radio's "Marketplace" and numerous local television and radio shows.

She is co-founder of the Women's Institute for Financial Education

(WIFE), a nonprofit organization with seven hundred members in four chapters. Ginita writes the quarterly newsletter for WIFE.

About the Author

Dr. Victoria F. Collins is a Certified Financial Planner with a doctorate in research psychology and more than a decade of experience in financial planning. She is author of the book *Couples and Money* (Bantam, 1990, 1992) and co-author of the books *Divorce and Money* (Nolo, 1992, 1994) and (with Ginita Wall) *Smart Ways to Save Money During and After Divorce* (Nolo, 1994).

She has been interviewed on major radio and TV shows, including *Good Morning America*, *The Phil Donahue Show*, *The Gordon Elliott Show*, CBS News and CNBC, and in publications which include *The Wall Street Journal*, *USA Today*, *Business Week*, *The Los Angeles Times* and *The New York Times*.

Victoria appears daily on her own TV program, *Money Minutes*, on Orange County News Channel and is a guest expert on the PBS series, *The Financial Advisors*.

A recognized leader in the field of financial planning, Victoria is a member of the Registry of Financial Planning Practitioners and is active in both the International Association for Financial Planning and the Institute of Certified Financial Planners. Her firm, which manages more than $150 million for its clients, is one of the top twenty independent financial advisory firms in the country.

Victoria is a well-known lecturer and speaker whose audiences include the International Association for Financial Planning, the Estate Planning Roundtable, various Chambers of Commerce, the Young Presidents' Organization and the American Association of University Women. She recently had the distinct honor of being a keynote speaker at the International Financial Planners Conference at Oxford University, England.

The Outline

List of Chapters

PART I: Charting Your Course
    Chapter 1   Retirement Myths
    Chapter 2   Where Are You Going?
    Chapter 3   Creating Your Retirement Plan

PART II: Countdown to Retirement
    Chapter 4   Investing for Retirement

Chapter Three

Creating Your Retirement Plan   21 Pages, 3 Worksheets

This chapter begins with a discussion of income needs in retirement, how to gauge the effects of inflation and how to minimize the impact of inflation.

The chapter analyzes the outlook for social security and the role it might play in retirement plans. Readers can use two worksheets to calculate their retirement income needs and the amount they must save to satisfy those needs.

The chapter then explains the "triple squeeze"—retirement planning while educating children and supporting parents—and proposes solutions for the financial problems that may result.

A worksheet helps readers identify and juggle their financial priorities. Readers learn to cope effectively with the emotional aspects of the "triple squeeze"—guilt, resentment, exhaustion, overload, fears and depression. They learn about helpful tools for setting priorities and boundaries and for communicating them to loved ones.

The chapter ends by counseling readers who expect to inherit money, and thus have less perceived need for retirement planning, but greater need for money-management education. The chapter cautions readers not to plan to retire on their spouse's retirement, because an end to the marriage through death or divorce could derail such a plan.

[Roger Crawford's proposal gave him the chance to show how he has been able to transform the misfortunes of his birth into a life of achievement to which people born without the benefit of his disadvantages can only aspire. With his charm, speaking ability and formidable schedule, which was included with his first-rate proposal, Roger made our job easy.

Part of the beauty of Roger's idea is its crossover potential. The need for resilience is universal. It's as important to corporations as it is to the nonprofits Roger speaks to. It's also as important in people's personal lives as it is at work.)

A Proposal for
How High Can You Bounce?
The 9 Keys to Personal Resilience
By Roger Crawford

Table of Contents

Introduction	
Overview	2
Promotion	6
About the Authors	14
The Outline	
List of Chapters	17
Sample Chapters	44

Enclosed separately in the folder:
The author's brochure
His speaking schedule for the year [which was four pages long!]
A partial list of the author's clients, speaking and media appear-
    ances, and articles about the author
A jacket of the author's previous book
Reprints of two stories about the author
A photograph

[Another major plus Roger brings to the project is a fun, up-beat, visual title that is perfect in how it captures the feeling for a book on resilience. At this writing, the subtitle for this book (pub date: January 1998) had been changed to *Turn Setbacks Into Comebacks*.]

Introduction
Overview

Some people are born survivors. Nothing can get them. They bound through life, actually gaining energy and momentum for the same pressures that slow everybody else down. This is because they have *personal resilience.*

People don't have to be born with this power. It can be *learned.* This business-oriented self-help book will show readers how to strengthen their own personal resilience so they can:

- regain stability more quickly in difficult situations
- stay physically and emotionally healthy during periods of stress and uncertainty
- remain hopeful and optimistic when others have given up
- rebound from adversity even stronger than before
- make life richer, more productive, happier and more successful.

Roger Crawford is unique, and *How High Can You Bounce? The 9 Keys to Personal Resilience* will have a unique message. *How High* will be the first book to describe the nine characteristics of highly resilient people and show readers how to acquire them by building on skills and attitudes they already have to achieve optimum resiliency.

Each chapter will be full of the author's extraordinary personal anecdotes as he shows how to exercise attitudinal muscles the same way one exercises physical muscles. As a physically challenged champion athlete, Roger Crawford has had plenty of experience doing both.

As an internationally acclaimed motivational speaker, he knows how to touch minds and hearts while providing practical, easy-to-follow instructions that can improve productivity, increase pleasure and change people's lives.

How High Can You Bounce? will be 253 pages with an introduction; three sections containing three chapters each about the nine keys; a conclusion, a two-page bibliography and an index.

Each of the three sections will have a two-page introduction and explore a different theme. Each of the nine chapters will include a(n):

- strong, humorous opening story about one of Roger's personal experiences

- inspirational profile of someone who symbolizes each key
- Skill Builder section, with exercises and quizzes to demonstrate and strengthen the reader's current abilities
- summary of key points in the chapter and a humorous closing anecdote.

Spin-offs

The author will write two follow-up books:

- *The Resilient Leader.* Roger is already gathering material for this sequel. In his dozen years of speaking around the United States and the world, Roger has frequently seen resilient leadership in action. These enlightening and inspiring stories will make a strong business book.
- *The Resilient Salesperson.* Few careers require more resilience than selling. About 15 percent of the American workforce is involved in sales. That makes nineteen million potential buyers.

Promotion

The author will help the publisher promote the book in the following twelve ways:

- **PR budget:** Roger will match the publisher's consumer promotion budget up to $_____.
- **Coordinated publicity tour:** Roger will contact local newspapers and TV and radio stations in the more than one hundred cities he visits annually to set up interviews about his book.
- **Pre-sold books:** Roger will purchase _____ or more books a year for four years.
- **Mailing list:** Roger has a database with more than thirteen thousand of the people who purchased his first book, *Playing From the Heart.* He will pre-sell autographed copies of *How High Can You Bounce?* prior to its release.

[The list of quotes that Roger will obtain proves that he has a solid professional network.]

- **Endorsements:** Roger will obtain quotes about the book from ESPN anchor Robin Roberts; top motivational speakers/authors Zig Ziglar, author of *See You at the Top,* and Og Mandino, author of *The Greatest Salesman in the World*; former New York Knicks basketball coach Pat Riley; Dr. Wayne Dyer, author of *You Will See It When You Believe It*; Dr. Robert Schuller, author of *Possibility Thinking*; Nancy Austin, coauthor with Tom Peters of *A Passion for Excellence*; Denis Waitley, author of *Seeds of Greatness*; Olympic Gold Medalist Mary Lou Retton; and others.

Here are four early quotes:

> *"How High Can You Bounce?* is chicken soup for the resilient soul. If you desire to rise above your current level of performance, buy and read this book! Prepare to be inspired and empowered by someone who understands the incredible power of resilience, because he has lived it."
>
> —Jack Canfield, coauthor of *Chicken Soup for the Soul*

[You'll see in the bio below why Roger got a quote from Jack.]

> *"Roger Crawford is a great model of the resilient quality needed to excel in today's high-stress world. Read this book and you'll learn how to perform with grace under pressure."*
>
> —Dr. Robert Kreigel, author of *If It Ain't Broke . . . Break It* and *Sacred Cows Make the Best Burgers*

> *"Roger has captured the essence of that most elusive and essential quality for life, resilience. Even more remarkably, he proves that resilience can be learned."*
>
> —Alan Loy McGinnis, author of *The Friendship Factor*

> *"Roger Crawford is an inspiration to me. Inspiration means 'in-spirit.' His work, indeed his life, is in-spirit. Read carefully and be in-spired."*
>
> —Dr. Wayne Dyer, author of *Your Erroneous Zones*, *Pulling Your Own Strings* and *Real Magic*

• **National coverage:** *Good Morning America*, NBC, *USA Today*, CNBC, *Real People* and Dr. Schuller's *Hour of Power* are among the two dozen national and local TV shows that have already covered Roger's first book, and he has maintained the contacts. He has also done numerous radio interviews. Roger's humor and dynamic attitude make him an effective promoter.

• **Spin-off articles in corporate and association magazines:** Of the many organizations and associations that Roger has addressed, at least 150 publish a regular magazine or newsletter. To give the book maximum exposure, Roger will custom-tailor book excerpts from *How High Can You Bounce?* into articles and offer them to these publications. Each article will end with an 800-number that readers can use to order copies of the book. These publications will be very receptive to Roger's articles, especially since many of their readers have already heard Roger speak.

Six examples are the publications of:

National Association of Credit Unions, with more than 250,000 subscribers. Roger was its keynote speaker in 1992.

National Association of Life Underwriters, with 200,000 readers. Roger was the keynote speaker in 1993.

United States Professional Tennis Association, a monthly magazine that goes to 6,500 people. Roger is very well known in tennis circles, so an article should generate great interest in the book.

General Motors. Roger has spoken twelve times for General Motors in the past two years. He has already had an article in the company magazine (circulation 25,000) in 1993, which was very well received. A follow-up book excerpt should do very well.

National Association of Accountants, circulation 10,000. Roger was the keynote speaker in 1993.

The National Parents and Teachers Association, circulation 27,000. Roger has been the keynote speaker twice.

- **Spin-off articles in national magazines:** Many of the topics and anecdotes will make good short articles for publications like *Parade*, *Reader's Digest* and *People Magazine*. Roger has already been featured in and will approach the following three magazines:

Success
Personal Selling Power
Tennis.

- **Tie-in to movie or TV movie:** A film script of Roger's first book, *Playing From the Heart*, is being considered by several producers.
- **A PBS special in conjunction with the book:** PBS in Los Angeles taped Roger's speech before the Los Angeles County Teachers' Association and aired it as an inspirational program similar to those of Leo Buscaglia. Roger received more than sixty phone calls and booked ten speaking engagements as a result. Deanne Hamilton, former producer of the long-running *People are Talking* for KGO-TV (San Francisco's ABC affiliate) and now a producer for KQED-TV (PBS-San Francisco), is eager to see the finished book, and will assist Roger in contacting other PBS stations.

- **Corporate sponsorship:** Roger will send autographed copies of *How High Can You Bounce?* to organizations that are mentioned in the book, such as Prudential Insurance, Wilson Sporting Goods, and AT&T. This will encourage them to block-buy books for their employees and others. Roger used this technique with his first book, *Playing From the Heart.*
- **An 800-telephone number:** Roger will set up an 800-number for ordering *How High Can You Bounce?* and will mention this number in all publicity connected with the book, such as interviews, articles, handouts at speeches and mailings.

[Like Elise, Roger was lucky to have no competitive books when we were selling his proposal. Two did come out afterward, however. Roger was also lucky to be able to tie his book into a new trend in business books.]

Complementary books

This book is part of the new "kinder, gentler" school of crossover business books, focusing on how to acquire a permanent source of personal energy—a positive attitude—that is crucial to business success. Recent books appealing to the same audience include:

The Seven Habits of Highly Effective People by Stephen R. Covey, Fireside Books, 340 pages. A best-seller that describes the characteristics of highly effective people and offers step-by-step how-to information.

Zapp! The Lightning of Empowerment by William Byham and Jeff Cox, Fawcett Columbine, 200 pages. How to give unmotivated employees a "Zapp!" of excitement and positiveness.

The Goal by Eliyahu M. Goldratt, North River Press, 333 pages. A best-seller about discarding old solutions and applying positive new thinking to new problems.

The Pursuit of Wow!: Every Person's Guide to Topsy-Turvy Times by Tom Peters, Vintage Original, 330 pages. Survival skills for difficult times.

Making a Difference: Twelve Qualities That Make You a Leader by Sheila Murray Bethel, G.P. Putnam and Berkley paperback, 273 pages. On several best-seller lists and still selling briskly.

Roger is connected to another best-seller:

Chicken Soup for the Soul: 101 Stories to Open the Heart and Rekindle the Spirit by Jack Canfield and Mark Victor Hansen. Roger Crawford was a contributing writer. This book has sold 3.9 million copies as of June, 1995. That means that at least 3.9 million people already know something about Roger and should respond positively to reminders of Roger's chapter in this book.

[Roger's idea is so universal that he didn't have to say much about markets.]

Markets for the book

At least fifty million Americans purchase business, inspirational and self-help books each year. A practical, mainstream, no-nonsense guide to strengthen personal and professional resiliency will appeal to a broad range of book buyers.

The author will deliver the manuscript six months after receipt of the advance.

About the Author

Roger is the author of *Playing From the Heart* (Prima Publishing, 1989, with Michael Bowker). This inspirational story of how he met his own challenges has been especially popular with younger audiences.

A champion in the business world. Each year Roger addresses 120 organizations and more than 100,000 people. His enthusiastic clients include Adidas, Aetna, Allstate, American Airlines, Amway, AT&T, Blue Cross/Blue Shield, Chevrolet, Citibank, Coldwell Banker, Hewlett-Packard, IBM, Kraft General Foods, Metropolitan Life, NCR, Pacific Bell, State Farm, Travelers Insurance, Union Carbide and Xerox. Roger has made speaking appearances in all fifty states and thirteen foreign countries, including Germany, Spain, Canada, Brazil, Jamaica, Bermuda, Portugal, Mexico and New Zealand. He contributed extensively to the 1991 G.O.A.L.S. Program, still used by the state of California to motivate welfare recipients.

A champion on the courts. Despite his physical limitations, Roger holds certification from the United States Professional Tennis Association as a tennis professional. In high school, he was a four-year letterman in tennis with a 47 win/6 loss record. At Loyola Marymount University in Los Angeles, he earned a Bachelor of Arts degree in communications while becoming the first athlete with a severe disability to compete in an NCAA Division I college sport. Roger stars in tennis exhibitions and has teamed up with celebrities such as Joe Montana. In 1984, Roger carried the Olympic torch for one-and-a-half miles through downtown San Francisco.

A champion in life. More than a million people have come into contact with Roger Crawford—in person, on video or on the printed page. Roger has tried to change the way they feel about their own lives and options. His sensible, positive philosophy is highly contagious.

About Eleanor Dugan

Although Eleanor Dugan will not be credited on the cover, she will coauthor this book, converting Roger's presentation material into written form and supporting it with research on resilience. Eleanor is the author of more than a dozen books on communications and business subjects, including:

[An impressive list of eleven books followed.]
[The following list is a creative idea: an effective summary of the strengths Roger brings to the project.]

Why the author believes the book will be a success

Here are eight reason why *How High* will succeed:

- Roger Crawford is highly credible.
- He has the promoting and marketing experience needed to make the book a tremendous success.
- Roger's heavy calendar of speaking engagements—at least 120 a year—proves that his message is timely and salable, and guarantees continuing national exposure for the book.

He is represented by forty of the top speaking bureaus in the country, including the prestigious Washington Speakers' Bureau, which is the exclusive agent for George Bush, Margaret Thatcher, Tom Peters, Dan Quayle, Colin Powell, Lee Iacocca and Olympic Gold Medalist Mary Lou Retton (the only speaker on their roster younger than Roger).

- In 1994, 75 percent of Roger's clients were corporations or business associations, up from 30 percent in 1990. The remainder were educational, medical, civic and fraternal organizations.
- His first book, *Playing From the Heart*, received a unanimously positive response and is about to come out in paperback.
- The diverse audiences that the author addresses prove that the book will have wide appeal. In the first six months of 1995, Roger spoke to:

Thirty-five corporate clients (14,000 people)
Twelve business and civic associations (7,200 people)

Eight educational groups: students/teachers/principals/counselors
   (6,500 people)
Four medical groups (5,000 people)
One general public (1,500 people)
A total of 35,000 people in sixty different groups. (Please see the
   enclosed copy of his schedule.)

 • International exposure: Roger has spoken in thirteen foreign
countries.
 • Roger is thirty-four-years-old and plans a long speaking career,
so the book will have strong backlist potential.

[Another of the proposal's virtues that will appeal to editors
is the book's harmonious structure: The book has three parts
and each of the parts has three chapters. Roger chose to start
the outline with the text of his introduction, which, alas, we
couldn't include, to give editors the flavor of the book.]

The Outline
List of Chapters

[Roger's use of anecdotes at the beginning and end of each chapter gave editors a feeling for what the chapter would be like and

made the outlines more enjoyable to read. Roger didn't have one line of outline for the thirty-two pages he projected for the length of the chapter, but his anecdotes helped assure that editors wouldn't think his outline was "thin."]

Chapter Two

Use Humor   32 Pages

Fifteen thousand people still remember a charming, unintentional *double entendre* my wife, Donna, made in 1989. I was the closing speaker at the National Amway Free Enterprise Day in Ogden, Utah, sharing the platform with Les Brown, Dr. Joyce Brothers and Oliver North. (I was the only person on that platform that I'd never heard of!)

After my presentation, the master of ceremonies, Dexter Yager, saw Donna in the audience and urged her to come up and "say a few words." She was totally unprepared, but thanked everyone for their tremendous hospitality and then spoke briefly and eloquently about how important it is to see difficulties as challenges. She described how we had met and fallen in love, and how she had learned to look past my physical challenge to the real person.

She concluded, "Even though Roger is missing seven fingers and one leg, he's still the most fully equipped man I've ever met." The audience laughed for five full minutes. To this day, when we run into anyone who attended that convention, the first thing they mention is Donna's impromptu remark.

The core of Roger Crawford's message is humor—cultivating the ability to put a positive spin on negative situations. Flexibility is essential for resilience, and a sense of humor is essential for flexibility. This chapter includes illustrative anecdotes about developing flexibility through the use of humor. The chapter's practical skills include:

- reframing and redefining negative situations with humor
- using humor to handle change and to help others handle change
- getting people on your side through the skillful use of humor.

Profile: Harry Golden, essayist and editor of the *Carolina Israelite* during the stormiest days of the civil rights movement in the 1960s. Golden showed unique resilience, as he was right in the middle of it—a Northerner, a Jew and a liberal where any one of those qualifications could bring a midnight visit from men in hoods. His incisive humor clarified the real issues for both Northerners and Southerners, helped bridge the ideological differences and encouraged his readers to seek peaceful solutions.

The chapter concludes with a Skill Builder exercise, a humorous anecdote and a summary of the key points in the chapter. Here is the closing anecdote:

Airports are great places for people watching. Whenever I'm between planes, I try to find time to observe my fellow humans. One summer day I approached the only empty seat in the waiting area and found that someone had left a newspaper on it. My hands were full of luggage so I sat down right on top of it. Since it was a hot day, I was wearing shorts and a short-sleeved shirt.

A man was sitting across from me, approximately ten feet away. He immediately noticed my artificial leg and, a few moments later, my hands. He looked like he was desperately trying to conceal his curiosity. I could tell he was staring at me, because whenever our eyes would meet he would quickly glance at the floor or up to the ceiling. After a few minutes, he walked over to me. I anticipated he was going to ask me one of the questions that I've heard many times in the past: "Sir, were you born this way?" or "Were you in an accident?" But I was wrong, and I had to laugh at my own preconception.

"Excuse me, sir," he said. "I'm sorry to bother you, but are you reading that newspaper?" And I thought to myself, *what* kind of physical challenge does he think I *have*?

Chapter Eight
Develop Your Inborn Leadership Abilities   24 Pages

In 1993, my family and I were flying back to San Francisco from Albuquerque. This was a rare occasion when Donna and my daughter, Alexa, accompanied me on a speaking trip.

We had had a wonderful time, but when we got to the airport, we were really ready to get back home. As I approached the counter, I noticed something was going on. People were standing around looking upset, while a boarding clerk explained that the plane was delayed because of mechanical problems.

We were all pretty tired, but we understood. As I have always said, I've never had a bad flight because I've lived through every landing. Therefore, I always appreciate it when an airline takes the time to fix mechanical problems.

The delay stretched on and on. Four hours later we were allowed to board. We stowed our bags and buckled our seatbelts. The plane backed up about ten feet and stopped. Then the pilot returned the plane to the gate and apologized for the inconvenience: "Ladies and gentlemen, I'm terribly sorry, but I must cancel this flight." People around us were ranting and raving about the meetings they would miss and the urgency of reaching their destinations.

Back inside the terminal, people were shouting furiously at the boarding clerk: "I'm never going to fly this airline again!" One man said, "Why can't you fly even though the brakes are bad?" Apparently, he didn't care about the landing at the other end as long as he got there.

I realized it wasn't the clerk's fault and calmly arranged another flight the next day with the clerk. As I turned from the counter, a man approached me. "I heard you speak this morning," he said, "and I've been watching you for the last four hours. You told us about responding positively to negative situations, and I just wanted to see if you lived what you preach. Thanks for not disappointing me."

We lead by example. Leaders are always being observed, scrutinized and examined. As the old saying goes, "I'd rather watch a good leader than hear one any day."

Resilience must be shared. People who are not served well internally do not serve well externally. This chapter shows readers how to use the language of personal resilience to communicate optimism and resilience to others. Resilient people feel they have control. Therefore, it is usually possible to grow resilient people by giving them a sense of control.

Every leader is selling two fundamental things: solutions and positive feelings. The first is useless without the second.

Anecdotes will include how the Atlanta Downtown Marriott won back the baseball team that had switched to a less expensive hotel; how a remarkable school bus driver, Mrs. Torchianna, kept seventy-five energetic kids in their seats; and a poignant story about the time Roger met the man who had ridiculed and tormented him when they were children.

Profile: Ten years ago, on a bitter winter day, Flo Wheatly of

Hop Bottom, Pennsylvania, made an emergency sleeping bag for a homeless person. Now she heads "My Brother's Keeper Quilt Project," a nationwide movement of thousands of volunteers in dozens of cities that has produced and distributed more than ten thousand sleeping bags.

Skill Builder: a multiple-choice quiz for rating leadership behaviors and skills.

[P.S. Roger met with three editors in New York who all made offers. Once again, the winner was Toni Burbank at Bantam.]

BIBLIOGRAPHY

Adams, Jane. *How to Sell What You Write*. New York: G.P. Putnam's Sons, 1992.

The American Society of Journalists and Authors. *The Complete Guide to Writing Non-Fiction*. Edited by Glen Evens. Cincinnati: Writer's Digest Books, 1983.

Appelbaum, Judith, and Nancy Evans. *How to Get Happily Published: A Complete and Candid Guide*. 4th ed. New York: HarperCollins, 1992.

Appelbaum, Judith, and Forence Janovic. *The Writer's Workbook: A Full and Friendly Guide to Boosting Your Book's Sales*. New York: Pushcart Press, 1991.

Baker, Samm Sinclair. *Writing Nonfiction That Sells*. Cincinnati: Writer's Digest Books, 1986.

Balkin, Richard. *A Writer's Guide to Book Publishing*. 3rd ed. Revised by Nick Bakalar and Richard Balkin. New York: Plume, 1993.

Belkin, Gary S. *Getting Published: A Guide for Businesspeople and Other Professionals*. New York: John Wiley & Sons, 1984.

Bell, Herbert W. *How to Get Your Book Published: An Insider's Guide*. Cincinnati: Writer's Digest Books, 1985.

Billot, Diane ed. by. *Money for Writers Grants, Awards, Prizes, Scholarships, Resources and Internet Information*. New York: Henry Holt, 1997.

Boswell, John. *The Insider's Guide to Getting Published*. New York: Doubleday, 1997.

Burgett, Gordon. *The Writer's Guide to Query Letters and Cover Letters*. Rocklin, CA: Prima Publishing. 1992.

Charlton, James ed. by. *The Writer's Quotation Book: A Literary Companion*. Yonkers: Pushcart Press, 1980.

Cleaver, Diane. *The Literary Agent and the Writer: A Professional Guide*. Boston: The Writer, 1984.

Collier, Oscar. *How to Write a Winning Proposal.* New York: American Writer's Corporation, 1982.

Cool, Lisa Collier. *How to Write Irresistible Query Letters.* Cincinnati: Writer's Digest Books, 1987.

Corwin, Stanley J. *How to Become a Bestselling Author.* Cincinnati: Writer's Digest Books, 1984.

Coser, Lewis A., Charles Kadushin, and Walter W. Powell. *Books: The Culture and Commerce of Publishing.* New York: Basic Books, 1982.

Curtis, Richard. *How To Be Your Own Literary Agent.* Boston: Houghton Mifflin, 1983.

――――. *Mastering the Business of Writing.* New York: Allworth Press, 1996.

Dessauer, John P. *Book Publishing: What It Is, What It Does.* 2d ed. New York: R.R. Bowker, 1981.

Fife, Bruce. *An Insider's Guide to Getting Published.* Colorado Springs: Piccadilly Books, 1993.

Gaughen, Barbara, and Ernest Weckbaugh. *Book Blitz: Getting Your Book in the News.* Burbank: Bestseller Books, 1994.

Gross, Gerald. *Editors on Editing.* 3d ed. New York: Grove Press, 1993.

Gunther, Max. *Writing and Selling a Nonfiction Book.* Boston: The Writer, 1973.

Herman, Jeff. *Writer's Guide to Book Editors, Publishers, and Literary Agents.* Rocklin: Prima Publishing, 1997-8.

Herman, Jeff, and Deborah M. Adams. *Write the Perfect Book Proposal: 10 Proposals That Sold and Why.* New York: John Wiley & Sons, 1993.

Holt, Robert Lawrence. *How to Publish, Promote, and Sell Your Own Book.* New York: St. Martin's Press, 1985.

Kiefer, Marie. *Book Publishing Resource Guide.* 5th ed. Fairfield: Ad-Lib, 1996.

Kozak, Ellen M. *From Pen to Print: The Secrets of Getting Published Successfully.* New York: Henry Holt, 1990.

Kremer, John. *1001 Ways to Market Your Books.* Fairfield: Open Horizons, 1993.

Kubis, Pat, and Bob Howland. *The Complete Guide to Writing Fiction and Nonfiction.* Englewood Cliffs: Prentice-Hall, 1990.

Larsen, Michael. *Literary Agents: What They Do, How They Do It, and How to Find and Work With the Right One for You.* Revised and expanded. New York: John Wiley, 1996.

Levin, Martin P. *Be Your Own Literary Agent: The Ultimate Insider's Guide to Getting Published.* Rev. Berkeley: Ten Speed, 1996.

Levinson, Jay Conrad. *Guerrilla Marketing Weapons: 100 Affordable Marketing Methods for Maximizing Profits From Your Small Business.* New York: Plume, 1990.

Levoy, Gregg. *This Business of Writing.* Cincinnati: Writer's Digest Books, 1992.

Lyon, Elizabeth. *Nonfiction Book Proposals Anybody Can Write: How to Get a Contract and an Advance Before Writing a Book.* Hillsboro: Blue Heron, 1995.

Mandell, Judy. *Book Editors Talk to Writers.* New York: John Wiley, 1995.

McCollister, John. *Writing for Dollars.* Middle Village: Jonathan David, 1995.

Meyer, Carol. *The Writer's Survival Manual: The Complete Guide to Getting Your Book Published Right.* New York: Crown Publishers, 1982.

Mungo, Ray. *The Learning Annex Guide to Getting Successfully Published.* New York: Citadel Press, 1992.

Naisbitt, John. *Megatrends: Ten New Directions Transforming Our Lives.* New York: Warner Books, 1982.

O'Connor, Richard F.X. *How to Market You and Your Book.* Santa Barbara: Coeur de Lion, 1996.

Peterson, Franklynn, and Judi Kesselman Turkel. *The Author's Handbook*. Englewood Cliffs: Prentice-Hall, 1982.

Poynter, Dan. *Book Marketing: A New Approach*. Santa Barbara: Para Publishing, 1996.

———. *The Self-Publishing Manual: How to Write, Print, and Sell Your Own Book*. 8th ed. Santa Barbara: Para Publishing, 1994.

Roget's II: The New Thesaurus by the editors of The American Heritage Dictionary. Boston: Houghton Mifflin, 1980.

Ross, Tom, and Marilyn Ross. *The Complete Guide to Self-Publishing*. 3d ed. Cincinnati: Writer's Digest Books, 1994.

Strunk, William Jr., and E.B. White. *The Elements of Style*. 3d ed. New York: Macmillan Publishing, 1979.

Suzanne, Claudia. *This Business of Books: A Complete Overview of the Industry From Concept Through Sales*. Tustin: Wambtac, 1991.

Wilbur, L. Ferry. *How to Write Books That Sell: A Guide to Cashing in on the Booming Book Business*. Chicago: Contemporary Books, 1979.

Yale, David R. *Publicity and Media Relations Checklists*. Chicago: NTC, 1995.

INDEX